THE/

PLAYS THREE

Theatre Café
PLAYS THREE

HOLGER SCHOBER
Clyde and Bonnie
Translated by Zoë Svendsen

INGMAR VILLQIST
Helver's Night
Translated by Jacek Laskowski

RALF N. HÖHFELD
Busstopkisser
Translated by Vanessa Fagan

OBERON BOOKS
LONDON
WWW.OBERONBOOKS.COM

This anthology first published in the UK in 2014 by Oberon Books Ltd
521 Caledonian Road, London N7 9RH
Tel: +44 (0) 20 7607 3637 / Fax: +44 (0) 20 7607 3629
e-mail: info@oberonbooks.com
www.oberonbooks.com

PB ISBN: 978-1-78319-129-1
E ISBN: 978-1-78319-628-9

Cover artwork by Olivier Wiame

Printed, bound and converted
by CPI Group (UK) Ltd, Croydon, CR0 4YY.

Visit www.oberonbooks.com to read more about all our books and to
buy them. You will also find features, author interviews and news of any
author events, and you can sign up for e-newsletters so that you're always
first to hear about our new releases.

Contents

INTRODUCTION, 7

CLYDE AND BONNIE: Q&A WITH HOLGER SCHOBER, 10

HELVER'S NIGHT: Q&A WITH INGMAR VILLQIST, 12

BUSSTOPKISSER: Q&A WITH RALF N. HÖHFELD, 14

CLYDE AND BONNIE, 17

HELVER'S NIGHT, 69

BUSSTOPKISSER, 117

Introduction

Theatre Café gives a platform to brilliant new European plays that have had success in their country of origin but which have not been seen in the UK. Some of the plays have been written expressly for young people, some have simply caught the imagination of young people in their own countries.

Since 2004, Company of Angels and its international partners have run 11 successful and influential Theatre Café Festivals, presenting over 70 plays from 22 different European countries, involving 62 playwrights and commissioning over 40 new translations. Six Theatre Cafés have already been held in the UK, while international festivals have appeared in France, Holland, Estonia, Norway and Germany.

Our current programme of events, running across 4 countries from February 2014 to the end of 2015, celebrates Theatre Café's 10th anniversary, an achievement we are very proud of. Theatre Café Festival 2014-15 includes an International Youth Encounter for young performers from across Europe, and the European Writers' Lab, which will culminate in the creation of 4 new full-length plays by emerging playwrights from the UK, Germany, Norway and Holland. This programme has been delivered with the support of the Culture Programme of the European Union.

WHAT IS THEATRE CAFÉ?

Theatre Café is a theatrical space designed to create an informal, intimate atmosphere where audiences can relax and feel very close to a play. Every performance is followed by a discussion, with the playwright and creative team involved. There's room for audience involvement and also for the writers to benefit from the process.

I didn't know what to expect from a staged reading but I must say that the Theatre Café performance went far beyond what I dared to hope for. The setting itself made a very good connection between audience and actors, and the play worked perfectly in this atmosphere even though it is written for smoke, flying characters and a revolving stage. I kind of forgot it was a staged reading; the papers in their hands

7

became something like a concept rather than a reminder of words or text. Andri Snær Magnason (Iceland)

What Company of Angels does is so hugely important for the UK theatre scene; it is really a leading light when it comes to bringing European work to the forefront and also at finding ways of collaboration. Sissi Lichtenstein (Author's agent)

Company of Angels looks for European plays that are original in both form and style and with important stories to tell. They must also be plays that we believe speak to a wider public, beyond their immediate country of origin. Each of the texts in this anthology has featured at a Theatre Café Festival. They are each written for two cast members and demonstrate the sheer breadth of theme and content showcased by Theatre Café. *Helver's Night* by Ingmar Villqist (Poland) is an expressionist drama about Carla and her charge, Helver, who is fascinated with the spectacle and symbolism of fascism; *Busstopkisser* by Ralf N. Höhfeld (Germany) takes the audience on a tweet-sized journey through adolescent romance; while *Clyde and Bonnie* by Holger Schober (Austria) is a B-movie for the stage, about disillusion, unemployment, social deprivation, violence and love.

For over a decade, Theatre Café Festivals have become an indispensable way of moving plays and artists between different cultures and languages. We hope more and more European plays will be seen on UK stages in the next ten years too.

Teresa Ariosto
Artistic Director of Company of Angels and Curator of Theatre Café
October 2014

Company of Angels fosters and produces challenging theatre for and with young people and the adults in their lives. We nurture the next generation of artists. We bring plays, artists and ideas from Europe. We engage with a range of artistic forms within and beyond theatre making.

THEATRE CAFÉ PLAYS PRODUCED IN THE UK:

- *Truckstop* by Lot Vekemans (Holland), Edinburgh Festival and UK tour, 2007

- *This Child* by Joel Pommerat (France), UK tour, autumn 2008; ALRA, London, spring 2010; and Bridewell Theatre, London, summer 2013

- *Invasion!* by Jonas Hassen Khemiri (Sweden), Soho Theatre, London, spring 2009; and Tooting Arts Club, spring 2011

- *Sense* by Anja Hilling (Germany), Southwark Playhouse, London, spring 2009; Imaginate Festival, Edinburgh, spring 2010; Hen and Chickens, London, autumn 2011; and ALRA, spring 2013

- *Monsters* by Niklas Rådstrom (Sweden), Arcola Theatre, London, spring 2009

- *Respect* by Lutz Hübner (Germany), Birmingham Rep, spring 2010; and ALRA, London summer 2014

- *Colörs* by Peca Stefan (Romania), Tristan Bates Theatre, spring 2010

- *Blowing* by Jeroen van den Berg (Holland), UK tour, autumn 2010

- *Anne and Zef* by Ad de Bont (Holland), Salisbury Playhouse, spring 2012

- *Busstopkisser* by Ralf N. Höhfeld (Germany), Camden People's Theatre, spring 2014

- *Helver's Night* by Ingmar Villqist (Poland), York Theatre Royal Studio, from 30th October until 8th November 2014

CLYDE AND BONNIE

Q&A with HOLGER SCHOBER

Why do you write for the theatre?

I am a trained actor and I worked as an actor for about ten years, but I always felt that there has to be 'more' in my artistic life. I wanted to create and not to reproduce, so I started to write and later direct. Now I see myself first as a father, then a writer, then a director, and last as an actor. I also write scripts for TV, but in my experience there is a big difference between writing for the screen and writing for the theatre. When I write a TV script I am facing a line producer, who thinks he can do my work far better than me and that it would be better to live in a world without script writers. When I write for the theatre I am facing a dramatic advisor who thinks that I am a genius and will write a play that will be a revolution to the theatre. It is all about worshipping.

Do you think your play could work anywhere in the world?

Definitely! This play is about global topics, like unemployment, the quest for a place in this messed-up world, the one and only true love and about a system that is strengthening the strong and weakening the weak. These are thoughts which a lot of young people all over the world can share.

What inspired you to write this play?

I wrote this play in two days for a little Austrian theatre that wanted to give a focus to plays that deal with horror movies, B-movies, or with movies in general. They asked me if I had something in the box for that, and I said, of course. That was on a Friday at 12pm and they wanted to have this on the desk by Monday morning. So I sat down and wrote the whole play in two and a half days. It helped a lot that I grew up with B-Movies like *Teenage Bonnie and Klepto Clyde* and I had been thinking for a long time that there was some kind of new Great Depression coming up; I thought, if there is a new Great Depression will there also be room for public enemies like in the late 1920s? So I had the whole play more or less in my head when I started to write it. It was my 'luck' as an author that when we first produced that play in 2009, a big Depression was coming up, and suddenly we were the first theatre company that had a play dealing with the problem of the day.

What is the meaning of the multiple endings? Is there a 'true' ending?

Actually, I do not know. I think that an author is allowed not to know everything about his plays. There were so many productions of the play with so many different interpretations of the multiple endings, and I liked a lot of them, and I disliked many of them, but they were all possible and thrilling for me as an author. I think that is the thing about writing plays: there are a lot of other people involved, who put their interpretations, their thoughts and their histories into the performance, which – in the best case – means more than just words spoken on a stage. So I think the director, the actors and the audience should make up their own thoughts on what the endings may mean.

Who are Clyde and Bonnie?

Clyde and Bonnie are two totally normal young adults. They are dealing with a lot of issues which in my opinion are quite familiar. They come out of a childhood that was not exactly happy, but who doesn't? They have not found their place in life yet, they do not know what they want to achieve, but they definitely want to achieve something, because every human being wants to. They think the worst thing that can happen to them is that they die and nobody cares. You want to leave your footprints on the earth, because otherwise you have never existed. They had a hard time, but they are not white trash or something even worse. They are smart. They have needs. They have hopes. They want to achieve something that is bigger than them. So I think Clyde and Bonnie are actually you and me, all mixed up with the stuff that has got stuck in my brain in twenty-five years of watching very bad movies.

HELVER'S NIGHT

Q&A with INGMAR VILLQIST

Why do you write for the theatre?

I started writing at secondary school; some students wrote poems, others novels or stories, but I used to write dialogue and make up stories. I used an old German 'Erica' typewriter from the 1920's. I made my debut on the professional stage late – I was thirty-nine years old. Playwriting has always been my dream and then the dream unexpectedly came true, although I had never believed that it was possible. The prominent Polish artist Tadeusz Kantor once said, *'No-one who embarks on a life in theatre goes unpunished'*. My life over the last ten years has confirmed that, though I wouldn't change it for anything.

What does 'Europe' mean to you?

'Europe'... The word has been transformed in many different ways by Polish artists since 1989. Paraphrasing the words of the character from *Kartoteka* by Tadeusz Rozewicz, *'We in Europe... without Europe...under Europe...behind Europe... Oh, Europe!'* As an artist, I see Europe as a place to explore. There must be artists in every country who ponder the meaning of Europe. Or maybe not.

Do you think your play could work anywhere in the world?

Helver's Night has been produced over thirty times in professional theatres, as well as fringe theatres, since 1999. I think that's definitely an expression of interest. It has never been a hit. It is as sad as the lives of its defenceless characters towards the situation in which they find themselves. People like Helver and Carla have lived in many of the countries ruled by totalitarian dictatorships. So the play sparks interest, even though it is sad.

What has most struck you about this play's reception, in either your homeland or abroad?

It's been the lack of understanding for the story of Carla and Helver. There are plenty of plays about Nazism, fascism and communism, but few people have really got into the mystery of my two characters.

Can you say something about its dramatic form and language?

I knew that I had to create a unique language for Helver, to find a distinct rhythm, melody and turn of phrase. Helver's language reveals his inner world but also says something about the outside world in a naive language that is most honest and real. I wasn't thinking about any 'dramatic form' while writing. I was just as close as possible to my characters.

What made you combine the two elements of fascist unrest and learning difficulty?

Helver uncritically absorbs nascent totalitarianism and unwittingly diagnoses it by his admiration for it. Subconsciously, he picks up that discipline, brutality and order are the keys to survival. He wants to rescue Carla, so he teaches her.

BUSSTOPKISSER

Q&A with RALF N. HÖHFELD

Why do you write for the theatre?

I don't know. In my youth I liked the plays of the so-called 'Theatre of the Absurd', Beckett, French playwrights. So I started to write dialogues for myself, absurd, senseless dialogues. I liked it – and I haven't stopped writing since then! Of course, I hope that my dialogues are now not so senseless as they were at that time. Though I've never been a frequent theatre-goer, I like the 'live' situation. Real people playing, real people watching. Wonderful. I like to imagine people leaving the theatre after having seen *Busstopkisser* – and suddenly a boy kisses a girl. Or a girl kisses a boy. Inspiration! The magic of theatre!

What does 'Europe' mean to you?

For me, 'Europe' means: Wednesday. Football. In my youth, there was just one day in the week when all European Cup football games took place. There have been three competitions with wonderful names: European Champion Clubs' Cup, European Cup Winners' Cup, and the UEFA Cup. Watching TV on those Wednesday nights you discovered Europe, from La Valetta to Lisbon, from Reykjavik to Rome, from Belgrade to Barcelona, from Munich to Manchester. Every Wednesday was a lesson in geography. You learned more about Europe than in school. I wished to see all these famous and fabulous cities. But I wonder: what does it mean that my first impression of Europe is one of competitions, of battles, of winners, and losers?

Do you think your play could work anywhere in the world?

Yes!

What was your starting point for writing the play?

I tend to write plays about a girl and a boy. And most of these plays end with a kiss. A kiss does not always mean a happy ending, not at all. But after writing all these plays, I desired to write a play which starts with a kiss. A boy meets a girl and kisses her immediately.

Wow, what a perfect beginning! But then the problems start: what comes next? Seventeen more kisses and a whole play: *Busstopkisser*.

How did any research feed into the writing process?

To be honest, the research began after writing the play! In my experience, it normally takes eighteen months from first seeing a girl to the first kiss. Eighteen long months of desire, and suffering, and disillusion, and hope (so, in a way, the play has an autobiographical background). But after I had finished *Busstopkisser*, I was encouraged to reduce the time between seeing and kissing. And, believe it or not, it worked! It really worked! Last summer I met a girl – and I kissed her just five (!) months after seeing her for the first time! Incredible! We all should believe in the power of plays!

Holger Schober

CLYDE AND BONNIE

Translated by Zoë Svendsen

Further Copyright Information

Clyde and Bonnie

Holger Schober is hereby identified as author of this play in accordance with section 77 of the Copyright, Designs and Patents Act 1988. The author has asserted his moral rights.

All rights whatsoever in this play are strictly reserved and application for performance etc. should be made before commencement of rehearsal to Verlag Autorenagentur GmbH, Mommsenstr. 73, 10629 Berlin, Germany (theater@verlag-autorenagentur.de). No performance may be given unless a licence has been obtained, and no alterations may be made in the title or the text of the play without the author's prior written consent.

Zoë Svendsen is hereby identified as author of the translation of this play in accordance with section 77 of the Copyright, Designs and Patents Act 1988. The author has asserted her moral rights.

All rights whatsoever in this play are strictly reserved and application for performance etc. should be made before commencement of rehearsal to Blue Box Creative Management, Top Floor, 80/81 St Martin's Lane, London WC2N 4AA, Tel.: +44 (0) 20 7395 7520, (info@newbluebox.com). No performance may be given unless a licence has been obtained, and no alterations may be made in the title or the text of the play without the translator's prior written consent.

Characters

BONNIE

CLYDE

The action takes place here and now.

Zoë Svendsen's translation was kindly supported by Goethe-Institut London.

PROLOGUE

Interior/theatre/evening.

While the audience are entering the auditorium, Bonnie and Clyde practise their gangster moves in the mirror. We hear phrases like 'You talking to me?' or 'Where's the money?'. They try out different poses with their guns (angled Tarantino-style, or classically straight, or perhaps even one in each hand?). The audience are addressed directly every now and then – (eg. 'I'm sorry, am I bothering you?').

UNHAPPY ENDING

Interior/bank/daytime.

BONNIE: How's it looking?

CLYDE: Not too good.

BONNIE: Whaddya mean, not too good?

CLYDE: Not good at all

BONNIE: As in – ?

CLYDE: Cops as far as the eye can see

BONNIE: How many?

CLYDE: Too many. More than fifty.

BONNIE: What's the plan?

CLYDE: You take the hundred on the right, I'll take the hundred on the left and God can take care of the rest.

BONNIE: In other words, we've had it.

CLYDE: We're so far up shit creek we're practically out the other side.

BONNIE:	So this is it, then.
CLYDE:	More or less. More more than less.
BONNIE:	Famous last words?
CLYDE:	No.
BONNIE:	I love you.
CLYDE:	I love you too.
TOGETHER:	Rot in hell, you bastards!

Shooting.

ORIGINS

Interior/theatre/evening.

BONNIE: Clyde wasn't called Clyde when I first met him, I can't remember his real name – Walter or something – something with an A, anyway – maybe Werner, yeah, it was Werner – I fell for Clyde the minute I saw him. Bonnie was actually my real name, like that female mechanic in Knight Rider – my brother always fancied her. I preferred MacGyver – he was incredibly clever; you could learn loads from him. But Knight Rider was okay. Especially the episodes when David Hasselhof had that evil double who looked exactly like him except for a stupid moustache. Clyde had a moustache when I first got to know him – but in those days he was Werner, not Clyde. These days Clyde is cool. We're both cool. We make a cool couple.

CLYDE: Bonnie came in the door and the world sort of slowed down, like it was in slow

motion. You don't know what love is until
it hits you. It hit me so hard I thought I'd
never be able to breathe again. I still have to
take a deep breath whenever I see Bonnie
– Bonnie really is called Bonnie; parents
can be heartless at times. Bonnie's parents
were always heartless. She didn't have it
easy with them – I know that sounds like a
record getting stuck – who does have it easy,
anyway? But with Bonnie it's true, she's been
through a lot of shit, things no one wants
to hear about. Fathers whose fingers take a
walk under their daughters' skirts – that's
the sort of thing no one wants to hear. That
sort of shit does happen, and if it happens to
you it's not exactly funny. A lot of shit things
happened to Bonnie, but she doesn't let it
get her down – she never gives up. She's got
this sort of trust in things, in fate – always
thinks that somehow everything will turn
out all right – no idea where she got it from.
Does me good, anyway. Not something I
ever had.

BONNIE: It was like I'd been waiting all my life for
Clyde without knowing it. It's not like I
ever thought about it – about there being
anything else – I just kept on going. It wasn't
hard – before I met Clyde I didn't know
I was missing anything so I couldn't miss
it, could I? Life wasn't that bad – I mean I
didn't have it easy – I know everyone says
that, and maybe that's how everyone feels,
too, maybe it's just part of life, maybe it's
the same for everyone – obviously I only
know myself, so there's no way I can judge.
Sometimes things were pretty bad, but
somehow I knew that things would turn out
all right. And then Clyde came along and
everything changed. We met for the first
time on a Friday afternoon at about 3 p.m.
and at about 3.07 p.m. we did it on the back

seat of his car and then around about six or so Clyde said to me – we were pretty worn out by then – he said he wished time would stop right there and that we could stay like that forever – a back seat of love, which wandered the universe so we'd never ever have to be apart. I thought it was incredibly romantic. Clyde's always had a great way with words.

CLYDE: I've lost count of how many women I've had on the back seat of my car. There's been so many. But Bonnie was the first I made love to – it was something else altogether. For a second the world stood still and it was like everything around us had become totally meaningless, like we were in a super luxury suite in the Hilton and not on the back seat of a 1972 Ford. I knew there was no way I was going to let her leave, however high the price. And to my complete amazement she didn't want to. I'd never met anyone before who didn't want to leave once they'd got to know me.

When I was nine my father bought me a dog. That was the only nice thing he ever did for me; apart from creating me in the first place, of course. My parents hadn't been divorced long, I reckon he must have been feeling a bit guilty – at least, I never got anything from him again apart from a birthday card every couple of years or so. The dog was amazing – like a sort of little bobtail – like from that series, 'Here's Boomer'. I wanted to call it Rambo, but my mother wouldn't let me so it got called Baker, after Cheryl Baker, you know TV presenter, Bucks Fizz, 'You gotta speed it up, and then you gotta slow it down...'. Baker was a great dog. You couldn't teach him anything – he was too stupid – but if

your house was burning down he'd have
been in there like a shot, rescuing you. That
dog had a whole damn lot of love to give
and I had a whole damn lot of love to take.
Well, that and he couldn't open his tins on
his own and I had a tin-opener, so it was
probably cupboard love to an extent – still,
Baker was my best friend. But one day Baker
disappeared – he just didn't come home. We
looked for him for weeks – we even handed
out flyers about him – I put up the money
I'd been saving from my mowing job for
three years as a reward; I'd been planning
to buy a BMX bike. It wasn't much, but it
was all I had. I never saw Baker again. My
mother said he probably got run over by
a car and whoever it was threw his body
into the woods. She said it was all part of
growing up and it wouldn't be the first time I
lost someone I loved. She said she wouldn't
be around forever either and I should get
used to it. Having people who love you is a
luxury and you should enjoy it while it lasts,
but you can't rely on it. In the end you're
always alone.

Six months later my mother died in a car
accident. She had right of way but a man in
a silvery grey BMW ran straight into her. He
was way over the limit, although at the trial
he said he'd only drunk a couple of beers.
The steering column of her little Toyota went
right through her ribcage – she died at the
scene. The fireman who tried to cut her out
of the wreck told me later that her last words
were 'keep your head down'. Weird what
goes through your mind as you're bleeding
to death. What's really odd is I can hardly
remember what she looked like any more,
but I miss Baker all the time.

BONNIE: Clyde's been through a lot, I mean it's

25

not funny losing your mum when you're nine. It probably wouldn't be when you're older, either. Can't ever be much fun losing someone – I don't know why I'm talking about it being fun. Clyde's father didn't want him, I think he was quite cut up about it; anyway he never mentions him or if he does he just takes the piss. I've never lost anyone I was close to – that's probably partly because Clyde's the only person I've ever really been close to. When I was about fifteen my grandmother died and I went to her funeral. The weather was terrible, like in a bad film. My parents had booked a wind band who marched behind the coffin sounding a bit like a Bavarian beer tent at half two in the morning. At the back there was a guy who played the tuba, he had cerebral palsy or something, anyway his left foot was all twisted and the right side of his mouth hung down and he held his tuba all funny, sort of contorted. Looked like he'd be next in line for a wind band marching behind his coffin, anyway. I remember thinking that it was probably the cycle of life. A right philosopher I was in those days. It pissed it down, anyway, and the priest lost his place, because the rain made the ink run on his notes and he couldn't read my grandmother's name. I saw my Dad cry for the first and only time. My sister cried, my cousins cried, and a woman I'd never seen in my life before came up to me and gave me a hug and cried on my shoulder and told me I had to be a brave girl now. I tried and tried – I really put the effort in – but I couldn't cry. When my grandfather died it was the same. I thought about all sorts of sad stuff, like in Bambi when Bambi's mother gets shot. It made me cry buckets I was little – but even that didn't work. When my other grandmother died I didn't even go to the funeral because I was embarrassed about being the only one who didn't cry. I used to ask myself if it made me a bad person, if I was just cold and unfeeling – like if I was selfish and if other people didn't mean anything to me. Maybe it's partly to do with the fact that I always let life just sort of wash over me. When Clyde told me the story about his dog, I didn't stop crying for two days. Perhaps that's what it came down to. I've known loads of guys who've made me laugh. But Clyde was the first who made me cry.

CLYDE: I was sent to live with my grandparents – who I'd seen maybe twice or three times in my life. My mother didn't have a great relationship with them – actually my mother didn't have a great relationship with anyone really. My grandpa had retired, he was old-fashioned working class – you know the type – nose to the grindstone, honest, did his best for everyone. Just because you retire doesn't mean you can retire your attitude to life – so he carried on just the same – helping out anyone and everyone in the neighbourhood and all over the place – he was almost never at home. My grandma was probably a nice person, very quiet, a bit anxious, you couldn't really talk to her – but she was always there for you. I went a bit funny after my mum died – started messing around with firecrackers, bangers, all that shit – blew up tree stumps – and sometimes an ant's nest. My grandma wasn't too happy about it – I don't think she really knew how to handle me – so because she was at her wits end and because it had worked out well once before, she bought me a dog. A beagle. I was even allowed to call him Rambo. Rambo was a nice dog, could even do a couple of tricks that my granddad taught him on one of the

few occasions he was actually at home. I
think my granddad genuinely liked the dog,
and it made my grandmother happy to look
after something uncomplicated for once –
that just ate, shat, and slept. I didn't care
much one way or the other – I didn't mind
him.

One day though I got into an argument
at school – some shit like whether Knight
Rider or Macgyver was better – like there
could be any doubt – and some little ginger
twerp shouted at me like what did I know
anyway, orphans know jack shit. I punched
him so hard he lost two teeth – they were
only milk-teeth – and went home. I sat on
the lawn in front of the house and Rambo
came bounding up – he licked my palms and
looked at me with those typical doggy eyes.
I didn't want to be comforted by him – I
didn't want to be comforted by that good-
for-nothing stray – the only one who had
any right to comfort me was Baker and he
was long gone. So I went into the garage
and got some bangers from my store, which
I'd hidden behind a carton of screws that
my granddad never used – he never did
any DIY at home, only in other peoples'
houses – and went back out on the lawn
with Rambo. I stuck a huge firecracker
up its arse and lit it. The psychologist my
grandparents dragged me to see asked me
tons of questions but I didn't answer a single
one – not how he wanted me to, anyway.

UNHAPPY ENDING 2

Interior/bank/daytime.

BONNIE: How's it looking?

CLYDE: Not too good.

BONNIE: Whaddya mean, not too good?

CLYDE: Not good at all

BONNIE: As in – ?

CLYDE: Cops as far as the eye can see

BONNIE: How many?

CLYDE: Too many. More than fifty.

BONNIE: What's the plan?

CLYDE: Give ourselves up.

BONNIE: You asking me or telling me?

CLYDE: Dunno.
               You reckon they'd let us give ourselves up?

BONNIE: What do you mean?

CLYDE: We've only done in three police… It's not
               the sort of thing they forget, and if there's
               no witnesses no one will remember that we
               gave ourselves up. Everyone will have seen
               us draw our weapons, clear as day. We just
               didn't listen to reason – it's a tragedy but
               maybe it's better that way, people like us
               generally don't last all that long in prison.

BONNIE: The newspapers make a fuss for a week or
               so and then the pope dies or a cure for colds
               is discovered or we get thrown out of the
               first round of the Eurovision song contest
               and all that's left of us is photos in yellowing
               newspapers that some old grandma
               somewhere uses to line her birdcage with,
               and as the memory of us fades away our
               photos get shat all over by bright yellow
               canaries.

CLYDE: What a way to end!

BONNIE: Like in the movies.

CLYDE: Better.

BONNIE: Much better.

CLYDE: Popcorn?

BONNIE: Birdfeed.

CLYDE: Okay.

BONNIE: So what are we going to do?

CLYDE: Whichever way up you look at it, it looks
              pretty much the same.

BONNIE: The two of us in a pool of blood…

CLYDE: …hand in hand…

BONNIE: …surrounded by policemen….

CLYDE: …forensics taking photos…

BONNIE: …then they put us in two black sacks…

CLYDE: …and the zip is pulled up over your face…

BONNIE: …then over yours…

CLYDE: …they burn our bodies…

BONNIE: …and our ashes are strewn across the city…

CLYDE: …and we'll be one…

BONNIE: A good send-off.

CLYDE: Apart from us being dead.

BONNIE: Death's just the beginning.

CLYDE: Who says?

BONNIE: Yoda does.

CLYDE: Well if it's Yoda saying it… He should know.

BONNIE: Are you ready?

CLYDE: Are you?

BONNIE: Yes.

CLYDE: Me too.

BONNIE: May the force be with you.

CLYDE: Amen.

BONNIE: You're mixing your quotes again.

CLYDE: That's just my style.

BONNIE: You don't have a 'style'.

CLYDE: Who says?

BONNIE: I do!

CLYDE: Looks like I'm with the wrong woman.

BONNIE: Liar!

CLYDE: I love you.

BONNIE: I love you too.

TOGETHER: Rot in hell, you bastards!

Shooting.

LOVE STORY

Interior/video hire shop/daytime.

BONNIE: This one's pretty cool. Though I don't really
            rate Gwyneth Paltrow.

CLYDE: Why not?

BONNIE: I don't know – I can't take her seriously.
            I don't know why people make such a fuss
            about her.

CLYDE: I think she's pretty okay.

BONNIE: She's not pretty either.

CLYDE: I don't know…

BONNIE: Who *are* you?

CLYDE: Are you asking me an existential question?

BONNIE: No. I don't know. No.

CLYDE: Or are you just trying to get your facts
            straight?

BONNIE: I like you.

CLYDE: Are you always this upfront?

BONNIE: No. Never, actually. Only when it really
            matters.

CLYDE: And to what do I owe this honour?

BONNIE: I like you.

CLYDE: You mean my physique?

BONNIE: No.

CLYDE: You know it doesn't always pay to be so upfront…

BONNIE: I'm not saying you're ugly or anything, but your 'physique' doesn't really do anything for me.

CLYDE: Thanks.

BONNIE: I mean it's not just that. I like you and that's all there is to it. As a whole. It's not something you can explain.

CLYDE: What's your name?

BONNIE: Bonnie.

CLYDE: I mean really.

BONNIE: That's my name. Bonnie.

CLYDE: Don't take the piss.

BONNIE: It's the truth.

CLYDE: Bonnie. Like Bonnie in Knight Rider?

BONNIE: Nah. Like the cool Bonnie. The film with Faye Dunnaway?

CLYDE: I see. The cool Bonnie.

BONNIE: So what's your name?

CLYDE: Clyde.

BONNIE: Really?

CLYDE: No.

BONNIE: Pity. I s'pose it would have been a bit of a coincidence.

CLYDE: Yes.

BONNIE: Can I call you Clyde anyway?

CLYDE: You can call me whatever you like. It's a free
              country.

BONNIE: Hello Clyde.

CLYDE: Hello Bonnie. Pleased to meet you.

BONNIE: Me too.

CLYDE: Yeah.

BONNIE: What do you do?

CLYDE: You mean like my job?

BONNIE: Dunno. Just generally.

CLYDE: Not a lot.

BONNIE: That's not a lot.

CLYDE: Which pretty much sums it up.

BONNIE: Do you want to do something?

CLYDE: Okay.

BONNIE: Do you have a car?

CLYDE: Yep.

BONNIE: Is it outside?

CLYDE: Yep.

BONNIE: Is it cool?

CLYDE: Nope.

BONNIE: Doesn't matter. Shall we go?

CLYDE: Yep.

GROWING UP

Interior/therapy room/daytime.

CLYDE: No, doctor, I'm afraid I don't know why I
                 killed the dog. I do know that you aren't
                 a real doctor but it makes me feel better
                 if I call you doctor because then it feels
                 like maybe you know what you're doing.
                 I don't know why you would trust a title, I
                 mean I was voted the student most likely to
                 end up in prison four years running. If you
                 think that's going a bit far, you should see
                 the other categories the school magazine
                 had. From 'the girl most likely to lose her
                 virginity next' to 'the boy with the most
                 disgusting spots' right up to 'the girl that the
                 least boys fancy'. If you think life's tough,
                 you should try my school. Still I never had
                 it in for any of them, I didn't see the point.
                 Most of the lads at my school who thought
                 they were so great now work for some
                 insurance company in some open-plan office
                 somewhere, sorting things for other guys in
                 other offices who sort other things without
                 ever feeling a thing. Hell. How bad can it
                 get, having a job that you care so little about
                 you never even get sick of it. They're dead
                 already, guys like that, they never lived.
                 Being liked at school, that was just twitches,
                 little static shocks – real life is something
                 else. That's why I never had it in for any of
                 them – no need, they were already fucked
                 anyway. I've no idea what made you think
                 that, Doctor – do you really think that
                 because I blew up a dog, I'm likely to kill
                 a person? I don't quite see the relationship
                 between cause and effect here – a dog's a

dog – it's an object, something you own. If I wanted to blow up my bathroom cabinet, no one would bat an eyelid – okay it might be a bit loud, but I wouldn't do it out on the balcony. Why? There isn't a why? Why should there be a why? You do what you do and if you don't do it, you do something else. Why? Just because.

LOVE STORY 2

Interior/car/daytime.

BONNIE: I love you.

CLYDE: Why d'ya have to go and say that?

BONNIE: Because it's true.

CLYDE: Looked like you got what you wanted.

BONNIE: I did, too.

CLYDE: So why say something like that?

BONNIE: Because it's true.

CLYDE: Shit!

BONNIE: What's up?

CLYDE: Nothing.

BONNIE: Have you got the time, by the way?

CLYDE: It's late.

BONNIE: We took our time.

CLYDE: I've taken longer.

BONNIE: Poser.

CLYDE: Liar.

BONNIE: Oh yeah?

CLYDE: Doesn't mean all that much to me.

BONNIE: What doesn't?

CLYDE: Sex.

BONNIE: Not how it seemed to me.

CLYDE: Yeah, it was different this time. Usually it's
            just exercise.

BONNIE: Keep-fit-fucking? Qualified for the Olympics
            yet?

CLYDE: No – I'm serious – like going to the gym.
            I turn up, I work out – for how long just
            depends – and then I go shower. When it
            starts to get boring you change the exercise
            or concentrate on a particular muscle group,
            like on your abs.

BONNIE: We still talking sex here?

CLYDE: But with you it was different – there was no
            schedule – I had no idea what muscle I was
            going to be using next…

BONNIE: Well if you ask me, we used pretty much
            every muscle…

CLYDE: You think I use too many metaphors?

BONNIE: No – I like how you talk.

CLYDE: When do you have to go?

BONNIE: I don't have to go.

CLYDE: So you want to stay with me, or what?

BONNIE: Okay, okay, I don't want to get on your nerves or whatever, all I said was I don't have to go. I can stay.

CLYDE: Then stay. It's your life.

BONNIE: You're a bit bonkers, aren't you?

CLYDE: I am not bonkers!

BONNIE: You are bonkers.

CLYDE: Am not… What kind of a word is 'bonkers' anyway?

BONNIE: I don't know – you're the one who should know, it's you that's bonkers.

CLYDE: Why am I bonkers then?

BONNIE: I don't know, it's the way you talk. 'It's your life', that sort of thing. Everything stresses you out – you can't even say that you want me to stay.

CLYDE: I don't want you to.

BONNIE: Oh you don't want me to?

CLYDE: No.

BONNIE: You just said you did.

CLYDE: But only if you want to.

BONNIE: 'It's my life'.

CLYDE: That's right.

BONNIE: Well I'll be going then.

CLYDE: Then go.

BONNIE: Nearly gone already.

CLYDE: About time.

BONNIE: Goodbye.

CLYDE: See you.

BONNIE: Take care.

CLYDE: Don't go!

BONNIE: What did you just say?

CLYDE: Don't go!

BONNIE: I'm not sure I understand.

CLYDE: Stay here.

BONNIE: Who says?

CLYDE: Me. Please – stay with me.

BONNIE: Is that what you want?

CLYDE: You're doing my head in!

BONNIE: Didn't take long!

CLYDE: Come here. The thing is, the minute most women come they leave.

BONNIE: You getting all philosophical again?

CLYDE: I'm just saying you're different. You came, but you haven't left.

BONNIE: Maybe I didn't come, maybe I only pretended to.

CLYDE:	Did you?
BONNIE:	No.
CLYDE:	Anyway I didn't mean it sexually, I meant it spiritually.
BONNIE:	You bastard!
CLYDE:	Like soul mates.
BONNIE:	You've got a big one, haven't you. Soul, I mean.
CLYDE:	You too.
BONNIE:	So what shall we do now?
CLYDE:	Do you want to stay a bit longer?
BONNIE:	Only if I'm allowed to come again.
CLYDE:	You can come and go as often as you want.
BONNIE:	And what if I don't want to go away at all?
CLYDE:	Then – then I love you too, I think.
BONNIE:	Hi, I'm Bonnie.
CLYDE:	And I'm Clyde.

GROWING UP 2

Interior/therapy room/daytime.

BONNIE:	I've never done anything like that before – like say something like that to someone, not to someone I didn't know – or to anyone I did, either – not that I've got all that many friends. Actually there's no one I'd really call a friend. They're just people you know

– that's not really a good way of describing
it, because you don't really know them – like
people you've seen around a few times and
are sort of beyond the getting-to-know-each-
other stage. They know things like what kind
of music you're into, but they don't know
what you're thinking about when you cry
yourself to sleep at night. Not that I do cry
myself to sleep at night, I've got a problem
with crying, like I already said. I don't mean
not to cry, but the tears just won't come;
somehow whatever it is triggers tears just
doesn't work. My stomach clenches, and
right deep down inside me I can feel an
indescribable sadness spreading but before
it comes to the surface there's a kind of
switch or something and I just can't cry,
even though I really want to. My best friend
– the only one I had – was raped in the bath
by her uncle and told me about it. I'd liked
to have cried then. My mother left and we
never heard from her again. I'd liked to have
cried then, too. My father said he thought I
wasn't actually his daughter anyway. I don't
wish I'd cried then, but I wish I'd had the
courage to say something to him, something
cool, something... don't know. Appropriate,
you know. I never could find the right words
at the right time. Even in school. Definitely
not in school. The other kids always took
the mickey, said I was a bit weird. One time
someone said my mum was a prostitute and
I laughed because I didn't know what it
meant. I've never had a problem laughing,
not that there's been much to laugh about
– maybe that's why. Laughing and crying
are not the same thing at all, otherwise I
wouldn't be in the premiere league for one
and bottom division for the other.

UNHAPPY ENDING 3

Interior/bank/daytime.

BONNIE: How's it looking?

CLYDE: Not too good.

BONNIE: Whaddya mean, not too good?

CLYDE: Not good at all

BONNIE: As in – ?

CLYDE: Cops as far as the eye can see

BONNIE: How many?

CLYDE: Too many. More than fifty.

BONNIE: What's the plan?

CLYDE: We take a couple of employees hostage, bind their mouths with gaffer tape, put our masks on them, tie them to the chairs out the back there so it looks like they are sitting normally and turn the CCTV back on so that the cops can see both of them sitting there. Then we walk out the building and tell the cops they let us go as a gesture of goodwill, and we describe two men, both Cuban – small and wiry – and we say that they're crazy, likely to do anything, and that the police shouldn't rush anything because they're threatening to blow up the bank and then we give a false address and then we say we've got to go home because we're traumatized by it all and then we leave and the cops are scared to go in 'cause of what we told them and by the time they realise what's going on we're in Algeria and are opening a little bar by the beach where we live happily ever after.

BONNIE: Good plan. Just one small problem.

CLYDE: What?

BONNIE: They saw you.

CLYDE: Who?

BONNIE: The cops.

CLYDE: When?

BONNIE: Just now.

CLYDE: How come?

BONNIE: Just now. When you spoke to everyone in the bank.

CLYDE: But I had my mask on.

BONNIE: Yeah, but you weren't speaking Cuban.

CLYDE: They speak Spanish in Cuba.

BONNIE: Whatever. You didn't speak Spanish, and you're not exactly small and wiry either.

CLYDE: You trying to say I'm fat?

BONNIE: What? How come? No one's saying that.

CLYDE: You trying to say I'm fat?

BONNIE: Calm down! What's got into you?

CLYDE: Am I fat?

BONNIE: That's not what I meant.

CLYDE: I'm not wiry, I'm not Cuban, not a Latin lover, oh I understood you all right.

BONNIE: But you aren't Cuban.

CLYDE: To you, maybe.

BONNIE: In reality.

CLYDE: I know lots of women who find me sexy.

BONNIE: What's that got to do with anything?

CLYDE: They don't mind whether I'm Cuban or not.

BONNIE: I don't mind either, I still love you.

CLYDE: Yeah yeah, even though I'm fat and ugly, eh?

BONNIE: I didn't say anything about you being ugly.

CLYDE: Only about me being fat, eh? Got ya!

BONNIE: You and your stupid traps.

CLYDE: Got ya! Got ya! Got ya!

BONNIE: You know what? If you're going to carry on acting stupid like this I'm going to leave. I'm just going to walk right out of here.

CLYDE: And the cops?

BONNIE: I'll tell them you abducted me and I've managed to escape; that you thought I was well sexy; that you went crazy because I wouldn't let you touch me so you took me hostage so that I'd be your horny sex slave and submit to your every desire, and that I've had enough! You see this arse, this delicious specimen of an arse? Once it was yours, but that's history – it's not your arse any more, it's your ex-arse, and this particular ex-arse is going to shimmy its way out that door and all you'll be able to do is watch from back here how it wiggles from side to side and how the cops can't take their eyes off it – while you stuff your fist in your mouth: that arse belonged to me once but I totally fucked up. I've lost that arse. And all you're thinking about as the special forces pump you full of lead is my heavenly arse and the coroner won't have a clue why the guy who's got one thousand three hundred and fifty-seven bullets in him has such a happy grin on his face.

CLYDE: You are, and always will be, a minx.

BONNIE: That's why you married me. Or will marry me one day, if we survive this shit here.

CLYDE: You can bet on that.

BONNIE: That we survive or that you marry me?

CLYDE: Both.

BONNIE: By the way, why did you want to escape to Algeria?

CLYDE: When?

BONNIE: You just said we'd escape to Algeria and open a bar on the beach and live happily ever after.

CLYDE: I was just thinking that everyone escapes to the Caribbean – and who'd think of looking for us in Algeria, you'd have to be a total idiot to go there, but sometimes stupidity provides the best camouflage.

BONNIE: You know so much.

CLYDE: Nah, I'm just clever.

BONNIE: And the difference?

CLYDE: It's massive. You can get knowledge, read up on it. But you can't learn being clever, you just have to be born that way.

BONNIE: I'm neither.

CLYDE: That's not true. You're very clever.

BONNIE: Oh yes? When have I ever done anything clever?

CLYDE: You got yourself the handsomest, sexiest, sensitive-est, most-likely-to-satisfy-you-est guy you could find. I don't know what you call it, but I call that pretty clever.

BONNIE: I have my moments.

CLYDE: You are one long good moment. You are the moment that changed my life – and you've never stopped since.

BONNIE: You really do love me, don't you?

CLYDE: You know that.

BONNIE: You love me. You want to kiss me. You want to make out with me. You want to cuddle up to me. You want to play doctors and nurses with me.

CLYDE: I do. It's all I've ever wanted. It's what I came into this world for.

BONNIE: Me too.

CLYDE: Do you promise to love me and honour me, for better or worse, until death do us part?

BONNIE: I do. And you?

CLYDE: I do.

BONNIE: Then I declare us husband and wife.

CLYDE: Amen.

BONNIE: Speaking of until death do us part, how are
                we going to get out of here?

CLYDE: We shoot our way out.

BONNIE: How's that going to work?

CLYDE: Have you seen Young Guns? Emilio Estevez
                and Kiefer Sutherland and a couple of others
                whose names you don't know are trapped in
                this house which is surrounded by Murphy
                Dolan's gang, with the army – there's six of
                them and a hundred or so of the others. The
                army set fire to the house and they can't see
                anything because of the smoke – so they
                start to chuck things out of the house. They
                throw a sort of trunk out and all of a sudden
                Emilio Estevez jumps out of it and starts
                shooting. Then Kiefer Sutherland runs out
                and tries to break through the army line and
                by the end they actually get away!

BONNIE: One slight problem – we haven't got a trunk.
                And you're not Emilio Estevez.

CLYDE: It's only a film anyway. We're real.

BONNIE: Right now we're more real than I'd ideally
                like.

CLYDE: But the principle's the same. We can do it.

BONNIE: I'd go anywhere with you.

CLYDE: And don't forget, if we don't make it, we'll
                always have Paris.

BONNIE: We've never been to Paris.

CLYDE: Shit. It was still great with you.

BONNIE: With you, too.

CLYDE: For Paris?

BONNIE: For us.

TOGETHER: Rot in hell, you bastards?

Shooting.

GROWING UP 3

Interior/therapy room/daytime.

BONNIE: It's funny.

CLYDE: What is?

BONNIE: We've been getting it on for about two weeks
               now and we've talked about everything
               – I've told you everything about me, and
               you've told me everything about you, and
               then we just happen to bump into each other
               here – at the same psychologist's as we've
               not told each other anything about.

CLYDE: If you say so. I guess it *is* funny.

BONNIE: Not just funny, weird.

CLYDE: There's a difference?

BONNIE: Not sure. Something can taste funny or
               weird, like a mushroom, and it's the same
               thing – but something *being* funny is different
               from it being weird. Although you might
               find something funny because it's weird…
               Why are there so many words that are

supposed to mean the same thing in theory, but don't in reality?

CLYDE: That's just what the world's like, I reckon. There's always lots of possible meanings.

BONNIE: Like us meeting here for example?

CLYDE: Exactly. It could mean that we are both schizophrenics, or that we're both manic depressive, or that you're schizophrenic and I'm manic depressive or that I'm schizophrenic and you're manic depressive.

BONNIE: Are you schizophrenic?

CLYDE: I am not. And nor am I, either.

BONNIE: I'm not depressed. Perhaps a bit manic sometimes… But I reckon I'm pretty normal, psychologically.

CLYDE: Me too.

BONNIE: So what are we doing here?

CLYDE: Maybe fate is bringing us together because there's something special in store for us.

BONNIE: Like we're meant to save the world from aliens or something.

CLYDE: Something like that. Maybe not as extreme. Like save a baby's life or save a dog from drowning.

BONNIE: What sort of dog?

CLYDE: Do you like dogs?

BONNIE: I love dogs. What sort?

CLYDE: A bobtail.

BONNIE: What's a bobtail?

CLYDE: Have you ever watched 'Here's Boomer'?

BONNIE: Used to be my favourite programme.

CLYDE: Really?

BONNIE: Yes. I loved it. That's what a bobtail is?

CLYDE: That's what a bobtail is.

BONNIE: Yep. We can get us a bobtail.

CLYDE: We?

BONNIE: Yeah – I mean, if you're all right with that, I don't want to cramp your style or anything. If you want I can look after the dog and you can come visit or whatever – and you can have him every other weekend.

CLYDE: No need, it's fine. I'd like us to have a dog. Together, I mean.

BONNIE: What shall we call him?

CLYDE: Dunno. Waldi?

BONNIE: That's so dull. Our dog should have a cool name. Like Rex. Or Rambo. Rambo's a great name.

CLYDE: You got anything planned for the next 50 years?

BONNIE: Why?

CLYDE: Just asking.

BONNIE: No.

CLYDE: Then don't.

BONNIE: Why?

CLYDE: Just asking.

BONNIE: Okay. How come you're here, by the way?

CLYDE: I manifest a lack of control over my socially unacceptable levels of aggressive behaviour. That's what they say, anyway. You?

BONNIE: As well as being a kleptomaniac, I have proved myself incapable of conducting normal social relationships. That's what they say.

CLYDE: What does he know…

BONNIE: Judging by all his certificates on the wall, I'd say everything.

CLYDE: Judging by what they know about us, I'd say nothing. Shall we go?

BONNIE: Is that a question or a suggestion?

CLYDE: It's our future.

BONNIE: Well in that case how could I possibly refuse?

CLYDE: You can't.

BONNIE: No I can't, can I.

LEARNING TO LIVE

Interior/theatre/evening.

BONNIE: We're good for each other, Clyde and me.

He's right for me and I'm right for him. That's all there is to it. No catch. We belong together. No need for some psychologist with framed certificates on his wall. We're happy together. People always talk about people finding their other half. With me and Clyde it's different, we aren't two halves, we're already a whole; there's no boundary where he stops and I begin, there's nothing in between. We are simply us. Us two.

CLYDE: Bonnie is one in a million. I know that every guy says that about the woman he loves, but with Bonnie it's true. There's no one like her, like she's the only survivor of some long-forgotten age. Sort of a missing link between luck and fate, between time and space, between a Clyde who's almost certain to end up in prison, and an untouchable Clyde who is way more than he's ever actually achieved, a kind of super-Clyde. Bonnie makes me perfect and I make her perfect. But perfection comes at a price.

BONNIE: I never did have any time for money. Never had any, either. I only realised we'd got the euro a month after it came in, I was that skint. I thought at first it was play money – I don't really read newspapers, not because I find it boring, it's just that I don't really want to know too much about all the shit that happens. And maybe it sounds silly but I'm not all that sold on reading all those adverts for things I'd never be able to buy in a million years. Money was never my strong point. Not by a long way.

CLYDE: I never had a problem with money apart from one thing: I never had any. Never missed it, either. It was only after I met Bonnie that I started to wonder what it would be like to have money – what if I

could buy her anything she wanted; what if
we could just take off somewhere; what if we
just didn't have to worry about anything? We
didn't have that many friends, but the ones
we did used to make stupid jokes 'cause of
the whole Bonnie and Clyde thing.

BONNIE: 'When's your next bank robbery going to
be?' 'The police were round asking after you
this morning' that sort of bollocks. So one
day Clyde just said

THE FUTURE IS OUT THERE

Interior/apartment/evening.

CLYDE: If we suddenly got us a whole load of
money, what would you say?

BONNIE: Whaddaya think I'd say?

CLYDE: Imagine us having a massive pile of cash!

BONNIE: And where's it supposed to come from?

CLYDE: I've got a plan.

BONNIE: I won't let you sell a kidney.

CLYDE: That's not what I'm thinking of... not
any more, anyway, though it might have
worked...

BONNIE: I'm not letting you sell your body, your body
belongs to me.

CLYDE: I'm not going to, anyway, all I'm saying is
it probably could have worked out quite
well...

BONNIE: No.

CLYDE: Okay, okay. But what would you say if we suddenly had a massive pile of cash without me having to sell a kidney?

BONNIE: Or any other organ?

CLYDE: Or any other organ.

BONNIE: And you're not planning on pimping me, or anything like that?

CLYDE: Nope. I promise you, neither of us has to sell our bodies.

BONNIE: Or be an 'escort' or shit like that?

CLYDE: Or be an 'escort' or shit like that either.

BONNIE: Nothing illegal?

CLYDE: Depends how you look at it.

BONNIE: And how am I supposed to look at it?

CLYDE: Depends what sort of moral standards you have. Let's take robbing a bank, for example. Bankers have been stealing straight from their customers' pockets for centuries – it's always been the same old story – since the middle ages. The whole world's living on credit.

BONNIE: Apart from us. We can't get any.

CLYDE: Everyone else though. You want a car you can't afford, right? So you buy it on credit; a four-wheel drive so you've got space for the kids, kids you can't really afford either – and then you take your kids and your four-wheel drive on a holiday you can only pay for by borrowing more, but then you don't want to stay at home all summer, hanging around your house with its massive mortgage – and the banks see it all. And because you're up to your eyeballs in debt they offer you a loan that pays off all your other debts, and you pay the interest on it until the day you die and your kids inherit nothing except a whole load of debts and a twenty-year-old four-wheel drive which hasn't even been paid off yet. The banks thrive on shitting on us and that's why it's not immoral to rob a bank because it's really our money anyway and anyway the banks are insured.

BONNIE: But then you're robbing the insurers and that's immoral.

CLYDE: People who sell insurance have no right to talk about morals.

BONNIE: Okay – I get where you're coming from. So what's the plan?

CLYDE: That's it.

BONNIE: What?

CLYDE: What I just –
You know: bang, bang. Balaclavas. Hold up a bank.

BONNIE: You're mad.

CLYDE: It's not exactly original – but what do you think?

BONNIE: You're mad.

CLYDE: You said that already.

BONNIE: You're mad. Hold up a bank? How are we going to do that – we haven't got a clue about how to go about it.

CLYDE: It's not as difficult as you think. Have you seen Point Break?

BONNIE: With Keanu Reeves?

CLYDE: Yeah.

BONNIE: He's cute.

CLYDE: Why do women always think Keanu Reeves is cute?

BONNIE: He's sort of sweet.

CLYDE: Sweet. Sounds like a small dog. Do you really want a small dog for a boyfriend?

BONNIE: No, but he's sort of, I don't know, interesting.

CLYDE: Keanu Reeves is a complete dork. He's thick as pigshit, and only showers about twice a week.

BONNIE: Like you then.

CLYDE: Got nothing to do with it.

BONNIE: You could shower more often.

CLYDE: Don't change the subject.

BONNIE: I'm not. You said that Keanu Reeves is stupid because he only showers twice a week even though you don't shower any more than that. People in glass houses shouldn't throw stones or whatever you're supposed to say.

CLYDE: I don't have to shower. I'm not sweet.

BONNIE: But you are cute.

CLYDE: I am not cute.

BONNIE: You are when you're angry.

CLYDE: Whatever. Point Break.
                    Hold up a bank. All that matters is that we
                    do it quickly. In and out in nineteen seconds.
                    We don't bother with the safe, just take
                    what's behind the counter – you sort the left-
                    hand side and I sort the right. As long as we
                    don't get greedy it's child's play.

BONNIE: It won't work.

CLYDE: Why not? Are you worried about morals? I
                    explained all that to you already – the banks –

BONNIE: I don't give a toss about the banks, I'm just
                    saying it won't work.

CLYDE: But why?

BONNIE: We've no get-away vehicle. Or guns.

CLYDE: We can run away on foot. And I already
                    sorted us for guns. Look.

BONNIE: Have you gone crazy? You've hidden guns
                    here?

CLYDE: They aren't real. They've got plastic bullets
                    – they look real though – no one will be able
                    to tell the difference.

BONNIE: So the idea is to hold up a bank on foot with
                    plastic bullets?

CLYDE: You got a better idea?

BONNIE: Do you mean in general or just in relation to
                    criminal activity?

CLYDE: It might work.

BONNIE: What might work is that they shoot us.

CLYDE: They won't shoot us.

BONNIE: But they'll put us in prison for the rest of our
            lives. And I suspect it's unlikely that they'll
            put us in a cell together.

CLYDE: They won't catch us.

BONNIE: And who might 'they' be exactly?

CLYDE: How am I supposed to know – you started it.

BONNIE: Don't you think as ideas go, it's pretty
            pathetic?

CLYDE: No more pathetic than any of my other
            ideas.

BONNIE: Well, that's a real weight off my mind.

CLYDE: Do you trust me?

BONNIE: I –

CLYDE: Do you trust me?

BONNIE: Sometimes.

CLYDE: Do you trust me?

BONNIE: Yes.

CLYDE: Then let's do it.

BONNIE: You know you're completely bonkers.

CLYDE: That's why you married me.

BONNIE: I haven't married you.

CLYDE: But that's why you will. You think I'm sexy. You
                want my children. You want to be with me.

BONNIE: I want to be with you forever. All right, let's
                do it.

CLYDE: Okey dokey doggie daddy.
                We'll be like Bonnie and Clyde.

BONNIE: We are Bonnie and Clyde.

CLYDE: Hang on a minute – we're Clyde and
                Bonnie.

BONNIE: We're Bonnie and Clyde.

CLYDE: Clyde and Bonnie.

BONNIE: Bonnie and Clyde.

CLYDE: There's already a Bonnie and Clyde. We've
                got to have something of our own.

BONNIE: We've got a dog – that's our own. The lady's
                name always goes first.

CLYDE: Let's talk about it another time.

BONNIE: Let's.

CLYDE: Bonnie – are you ready?

BONNIE: I'm ready.

CLYDE: Okay – here's the plan.

THE HEIST

Interior/theatre/evening.

BONNIE: The first time felt really strange. Clyde had
                bought masks for us – George W. Bush and

Osama Bin Laden – he said it was a political statement – since we were only doing it because of the fucking system; but I'm pretty sure that's all they had in the shop. The eyes in the Bin Laden mask were way too small so most of the time I could hardly see a thing – and about halfway through I got really bad claustrophobia. Clyde kept his cool – apart from being so nervous he shouted 'This is a bank rubbery' by accident. But no one really noticed anyway because they were all too scared. All in all I think we did pretty well.

CLYDE: Okay, it stopped being so funny when Bonnie tripped up over a chair. And when I had to use the regional director as a human shield because the security guy turned out to have a second gun, it could have easily turned nasty. And after all that it turned out we'd only managed to nab two thousand, seven hundred and fifty-three euros, which wasn't exactly the triumph we'd imagined. But all in all, I think we did pretty well.

BONNIE: What's really crazy is that the fact we had no get-away vehicle was what saved us. The police blocked off all the streets really quickly, but we were already home, 'cause the bank was only round the corner from us – we had reckoned that seeing as we didn't have a get-away vehicle we ought to go for somewhere not too far away, so while the police searched high and low for us, we sat at home watching the latest episode of *The King of Queens*. It was really funny.

CLYDE: So after that we always did it that way. The police couldn't work out how we could get away so quickly – they probably thought we'd got ourselves a former Formula One racer as a get-away driver, we were that fast. The truth was that we just walked out the bank, calmly put our masks in our rucksacks, and walked off. Invariably when the news got out a little crowd would gather outside the bank, and we'd quite often stick around awhile, gawping inanely like everyone else.

BONNIE: Once Clyde said to some police officer – 'Sir, I saw everything'. I swear my heart stopped. He told the police that there were at least three of them, maybe four, he couldn't be sure, but he thought it was probably Cubans. I really had to concentrate not to laugh out loud the way the policeman, all earnest, thanked Clyde and asked him for his personal details – when Clyde said his name was Franz Macgyver, I really thought I was going to explode.

CLYDE: We were just too clever for them. They always say 'don't try this at home, kids, we're professionals'. But hey, you don't need to be a professional to hold up a bank, because the police just don't have any imagination. All you have to do is keep your cool, don't let anyone panic, and it goes like clockwork.

BONNIE: It was just a game and we got damn good at it. It's fun to play, when you're winning. In this game the winner takes all – and the loser gets nothing. Nothing at all.

CLYDE: It was our anniversary. Our tenth bank. I got us new masks to mark the occasion: Data from *Star Trek* for Bonnie and Chewbacca from *Star Wars* for me – I know, I know, what can I do? – Bonnie's a trekkie, but I love her, nothing I can do about it. We all dressed up in dinner jackets – we could afford it, after all. We went into the bank and I said to Bonnie – happy anniversary – and Bonnie smiled at me and said good luck, Clyde. Then we started the show – by then we had the routine off pat. I say: Ladies and

Gentlemen, if you could be so good as to lend me your ears for a moment, I promise to return them. A little joke like that relaxes people, I always think. I say: Please don't put up any resistance otherwise I'll have to ask my friend here to shoot your head off. Keep calm and nothing will happen to you, and remember: the money is insured but no one can give you your life back. Bonnie says I always come across so sophisticated when I'm holding up a bank that it makes her crazy for me. I look at the time. 60 seconds. I look at Bonnie and say – all right honey bunny and she looks at me and says all right sugar daddy. I've no idea where the guy came from – it was all like being in a bad film. In bad films there's always some hero who appears out of nowhere and saves the day, and our hero sure had a great entrance. I turned away from Data, back to my side of the bank and looked straight down the barrel of a *Dirty Harry*-style .45 magnum – and before I have a chance to wonder why in hell anyone still carries such an outdated weapon the guy's screaming: put your guns down or I'll shoot. Then everything went into slow motion. I hear Bonnie scream – 'you pig!' And then I hear a shot. The guy sort of shuddered, grabbing his right side, and then he aimed at me again. All at once I remembered what my mother said to the fireman as she was dying, 'keep your head down' – and I do and in that moment I feel a whoosh of air 3 millimetres above my head. The guy had missed me – and I grinned at him – but then I hear a sound behind me like someone dropping a sack of potatoes. I turn round and see Bonnie lying on the ground and she's bleeding from the head. Then I feel something pierce my left thigh. The hero just keeps on shooting. I spin round and shoot him straight in the chest. Then again. Then I empty the whole magazine into his bastard hero's body until I see the whites of his eyes. Then I turn round and the world returns to its normal speed. I run to Bonnie, pick her up – she's still breathing. I carry her out of the bank and take her to hospital where they operate on her for five hours and she survives. Before the doctors can tell the police I get her out the hospital and we disappear and no one ever finds us again.

In reality, it wasn't quite like that. We didn't have real guns, just the sort with plastic bullets, remember? But Bonnie's still dead. It was our anniversary and the job went as it always did. We strolled out the bank, Bonnie first, she gave me a smile and got hit by seven bullets. Someone had pressed the silent alarm and the police were right round the corner. They didn't hesitate for a second. Bonnie crumples and I go into autopilot. I stumble back through the bank and somehow I manage to escape through the bank entrance. I don't turn back I throw my mask in the bin and go straight into the next bar and somehow I'm still sitting here now.

SEND ME AN ANGEL

Interior/bar/evening.

BONNIE: Hello stranger. Ever flirted with death?

CLYDE: Enough for today, I reckon.

BONNIE: Buy us a drink?

CLYDE: What sort of drink?

BONNIE: Don't mind as long as it's a double.

CLYDE: Okay.

BONNIE: Thank you, stranger. You come here often?

CLYDE: Yes, all the time. Although when I really think about it, I reckon this is the first time. No idea. All looks the same to me.

BONNIE: Bars?

CLYDE: My life.

BONNIE: Know what you mean.

CLYDE: Do you come here often?

BONNIE: I'm always here. What are you doing here?

CLYDE: I thought I might drink myself to death.

BONNIE: Wow – being shot isn't painful enough for you?

CLYDE: That's about it. And it's way too fast – where's the fun in that?

BONNIE: Well, enjoy yourself. Do you want to be alone?

CLYDE: No, you're welcome to stay. Makes no difference. Man's an island. Alone.

BONNIE: Not exactly a barrel of laughs, are you?

CLYDE: A man comes home and says to his wife – tell me sweetheart, why has the cat lost all its fur? And the wife says but darling you told me to shave my pussy.

BONNIE: Like I said. Not exactly a barrel of laughs.

CLYDE: Most people laugh so hard they cry.

BONNIE: Cry, anyway.

CLYDE: Better than nothing.

BONNIE: If you say so.

CLYDE: Ever thought about death?

BONNIE: Not really.

CLYDE: Why not?

BONNIE: I try and avoid it. If I don't think about it,
            maybe it won't think about me…

CLYDE: You're funny.

BONNIE: Well one of us has to be.

CLYDE: They say death's just the beginning.

BONNIE: Who does?

CLYDE: Yoda.

BONNIE: He'd know, I guess.

CLYDE: He knows fuck all. Did he realise the senator
            was evil? No. Normally nothing gets past
            him, but he didn't even notice that he had
            the evil Sith Lord sitting right next to him.
            He knew fuck all. Death is death, that's all.
            When you're gone, you're gone and that's it.

BONNIE: Have you lost someone?

CLYDE: Nooooo. I drink because I enjoy it and I
            enjoy it because I drink.

BONNIE: You lost someone, and now you've found
            someone, that's just how life goes.

CLYDE: Where are you from?

BONNIE: Here.

CLYDE: I've never seen you before.

BONNIE: Maybe you just weren't looking carefully enough.

CLYDE: Do we know each other?

BONNIE: Yes.

CLYDE: How?

BONNIE: From before.

CLYDE: Right.

BONNIE: Do you want to come with me?

CLYDE: Where to?

BONNIE: Anywhere.

CLYDE: Better than here?

BONNIE: Anywhere's better than here.

CLYDE: Will we come back?

BONNIE: No.

CLYDE: Okay.

UNHAPPY ENDING – THE END

Interior/bank/day.

BONNIE: How's it looking?

CLYDE: Not too good.

BONNIE: Whaddya mean, not too good?

CLYDE: Not good at all

BONNIE: As in – ?

CLYDE: Cops as far as the eye can see

BONNIE: How many?

CLYDE: Too many. More than fifty.

BONNIE: What's the plan?

CLYDE: You take the hundred on the right, I'll take
             the hundred on the left and God can take
             care of the rest.

BONNIE: In other words, we've had it.

CLYDE: We're so far up shit creek we're practically
             out the other side.

BONNIE: So this is it, then.

CLYDE: More or less. More more than less.

BONNIE: Famous last words?

CLYDE: No.

BONNIE: Will you promise me something?

CLYDE: Yes.

BONNIE: Don't promise before you know what it is.

CLYDE: I promise you anything you want.

BONNIE: Listen first, then decide.

CLYDE: Okay.

BONNIE: If one of us dies…

CLYDE: Don't start on that…

BONNIE: …If one of us dies then we've each got to take the other one with us.

CLYDE: What do you mean?

BONNIE: We belong together. We are one. If one of us goes then we should take the other one too. Do you promise me that you'll take me with you if you go?

CLYDE: I'll take you with me wherever I go.

BONNIE: Good.

CLYDE: Will you promise me that too?

BONNIE: I'll take you with me wherever I go.

CLYDE: Good.

BONNIE: You know sometimes I think that dying can't be all that bad. Maybe it's like a big party where you've drunk too much but when you wake up the next morning you don't have a hangover and you don't have to tidy up.

CLYDE: Yeah, maybe there's something beautiful about dying.

BONNIE: I reckon so.

CLYDE: I love you Bonnie.

BONNIE: I love you Clyde.

TOGETHER: Rot in hell you bastards!

Fade out.

Credits.

The End.

Ingmar Villqist

HELVER'S NIGHT

Translated by Jacek Laskowski

Further Copyright Information

Characters

HE

SHE

Company of Angels funded two research-and-development presentations for inclusion at Theatre Café Festival York in February 2014. Hal Chambers and Zoe Squire shared their excerpt of *Helver's Night*, going on to develop the full show with Company of Angels and York Theatre Royal, playing at the York Theatre Royal Studio, 30th October – 8th November 2014.

The stage is a working-class or poor-bourgeois kitchen. A fairly high-ceilinged space, kitchen furniture – a mixture of styles from the turn of the century through to the thirties. The front door from the stairwell is on the left, it opens outwards. There are three hooks on the inside of the door and on them are a man's coat, a woman's coat, a hat, a shopping net bag. On the right of the door is a large window with a wide sill; the outside of the frame is painted red, the inside – white; standing on the sill are a flower in a pot, tins, knick-knacks. Under the window is a wide, wooden trunk covered by a white cloth. In the wall facing the auditorium, on the left, is the door leading to a room; it's white and the top half has a rectangular pane of glass with a curtain. Above the door is a 'hunting' reproduction in a gilt frame. On the right of the door is a white kitchen dresser; on the dresser's plate a metal bread bin, enamel mugs, a large metal alarm clock and so on. The glass doors of the upper cupboards are covered by small curtains. There are large tins, a faience bowl, a large thirties radio set on the dresser. Against the wall on the right of the auditorium is a small gas stove, and on it pans with a prepared dinner, above the stove a small cupboard. A small wall-table between the stove and a cast-iron sink. Above the table – a calendar. Over the sink – an oval mirror in a metal frame. Standing in the middle is a white kitchen table covered by oil-cloth. On the table there are newspapers, mugs, two places set for dinner. Three white chairs, two small stools. The floor's boards have been painted red with oil paint.

The play is set in the kitchen of a one-roomed apartment in a working-class or poor-bourgeois district of a large industrial town in Europe.

Early evening. SHE is working by the gas stove, heating the dinner, waiting for HIM. Time and again she goes up to the door and listens. She goes up to the window, opens one of its wings, and looks out into the street. The swelling and growing sounds of a street demonstration can be heard. A crowd of people is approaching along the street. But not just along this street. The sound of marching masses can be heard spilling out over the whole district – increasingly loudly – the noise of boots on the cobbled streets and the paved sidewalks, shouts, chants, the crash of smashed glass – a moving wave of people approaches the window. She closes the window and gently retreats. She is uneasy – she senses danger. The sounds of the crowd under the window – very loud.

She withdraws a few steps from the window and stands next to the door.

She listens and waits. The loud bang of the tenement entrance door is heard; the sound of people running, of shouts, singing, chanting.

After a while the sound of stamping feet as someone runs up the wooden steps of the stairway. She waits, looking at the door. After a moment very energetic knocking at the door can be heard, and the door opens suddenly fully. HE runs into the kitchen, breathless, panting, covered in sweat. He is wearing well-worn but shining knee-boots, brown riding breeches, a belt with a silver buckle, a white, short-sleeved shirt buttoned at the collar, a leather Sam Browne, a black beret with silver insignia, he is holding a furled banner in his hand.

Kitchen. Evening. It is grey outside the window. The constant sound of rising then falling noises of the demonstration.

HE is standing a step away from the door. He is looking at her. Animated, hot, excited. SHE looks at him, calmly waiting. He slams the door with a bang and puts on the light, turning the switch to the right of the door frame. The bulb under a flat brass lampshade above the kitchen table goes on.

HE: *(Excited, feverish look, nervous, rapid movements.)* D'you know…?

SHE: *(Very calmly, keeping herself under control, though she senses something bad.)* Good evening, darling. I'm so glad you're back at last…

HE: D'you know…? *(Points to the window with his banner.)* D'you know what's happening? Everyone! I'm telling you, everyone's…

SHE: Put that down… *(Indicates the banner.)* And take off your beret. I'll serve dinner… Wash your hands, please. *(She goes up to the stove, picks up the pot using a cloth oven glove, carries it over to the table, pours the soup into the bowls.)* Well, sit down, please.

HE: *(Doesn't move from his spot; tense, twitching, observing her movements cautiously.)* Look out of the window! The whole district! I'm telling you, the whole district!

SHE: *(Goes up to the window and slams it shut.)* Let's sit down… *(Waits for a moment then sits down herself.)* Are you going to eat?

HE: *(Provocatively.)* No.

SHE: *(Starts to eat her soup.)* It's something you like – potato soup. Try it…

HE: *(One step towards her.)* Look what they gave me…
(He stretches the banner out towards her.)

SHE: I used smoked bacon and marjoram.

HE: *(Another step.)* Look! They gave me a banner. See? Not everyone got one…

SHE: *(Tasting the soup.)* Mmmm, it's delicious… I think I might have some more…

HE: *(Goes up to the window rapidly, opens it wide – the loud roar of the crowds.)* Look! *(Leans a long way out of the window.)* … E aaaa!!! E aaaa!!! *(Shouts to the crowds in the street.)* E eeee!!! E eeee!!!

SHE stands up from the table very slowly, goes up to him and puts her hand gently on his shoulder.

HE: *(Feeling her touch, he jumps back from the window and looks at her, confused.)* What?!

SHE: *(Calming him.)* Don't lean out like that, this is the second floor… Come on… *(Tries to take him by the arm.)* We'll have our dinner… You must be hungry…

HE: *(Accentuating each syllable.)* Don't you understand anything? No, you don't, do you? *(Keeps turning towards the window.)* Everyone is out there! Look! *(Leans out of the window.)* A aaa!!! A aaa!!! Go on, shout! A aaa!!! *(Waves his banner.)*

SHE: Let's leave it now… *(Gently pulls him away from the window.)* You're all hot… We'll eat, then you can get changed…

HE: *(Tears himself away energetically.)* I don't want to get changed, I won't eat… Besides, I've eaten already…

SHE: *(Sits down at the table and very slowly finishes her soup.)* What did you eat?

HE: *(Confrontationally.)* Pea soup.

SHE: Was it good?

HE: It was… *(Rapidly.)* I tell you, when we were all standing in the square outside the post office in rows… You know, I was standing in the very first row, like this… *(Shows her.)* Then right away they started to give out the torches, but Gilbert said that we weren't to light them right away, he said we'd light them when the groups from the north districts joined us and we'd light them when it was dark and then we'd all go together and then the field kitchens arrived, you know, the ones with the small chimneys, that was our garrison brought them specially for us so we wouldn't be hungry and everyone got a mess-tin and a spoon, and the cook who was pouring out the pea-soup gave me two ladles, you know, two ladles, and there were whole loads of bread, everyone could take as much as they liked…

SHE: And was the pea-soup nice?

HE: *(More slowly.)* And then they gave out schnapps…

SHE eats in silence.

HE: *(Even more slowly.)* I got some, too… *(More quickly.)* They poured it out of these big green thermos flasks… *(Slower.)* But only one… *(More quickly.)* 'Cause there was such a crowd that we were standing like this, right next to each other, right next to each other… And Gilbert said to me: 'Here, have some schnapps, go on, drink it.'

SHE: *(Stands up, goes up to the stove.)* Do you like Gilbert? *(She brings the dishes with the second course over to the table.)*

HE: Um, Gilbert always says: 'We'll make a soldier of you one day, yes we will.' And while we were standing there like that, Gilbert gave me a beret… *(Pulls the beret off and pushes it under her nose on his extended hand.)* See? And he pinned the badge on for me himself. See? He took it off this fat dummy who works in the laundry and pinned it to my beret himself. See?

SHE: It's a very nice beret. It really suits you…

HE: Right. *(Puts on the beret.)* And Gilbert gave me a banner, too. See? He told me to hold it like this… *(Shows her.)* Over your shoulder…

SHE: And didn't he give you a torch?

HE: *(Uneasy.)* No… *(To her.)* Why?

SHE: I don't know. Did you ask Gilbert?

HE: No, he was talking to some officers. *(Rapidly.)* And they were standing as straight as posts, you know. *(Shows her.)* They stood like this, and they did like this with their gloves against their hands – against their hands, and they were smoking cigars and Gilbert was smoking with them, and they had helmets, and they had swords, and one of them had, right here, in his eye *(Shows her.)* he had a spectacle, and this spectacle was on a string… he had this spectacle…

SHE: Monocle.

HE: Right. Why didn't he give me a torch?

SHE: I don't know. Maybe only the top people got them, so they could be seen better.

HE: Exactly… And afterwards Gilbert still smiled at me… And he praised me because my boots were well polished and he said an officer's boots must always shine like a dog's bollocks. *(More slowly.)* That's what Gilbert said, he said you could shave in boots like that, I'm going to shave, I think I'll shave today, because I'm going to start shaving, you know.

SHE: Good. Tomorrow we'll go and buy you some special soap, a bowl, a big flask of cologne and a razor.

HE: I'm going to use a cut-throat to shave with.

SHE: All right, we'll buy you a cut-throat razor. I saw a very smart one in that little shop next to the tram stop, it had a black ebony handle…

HE: *(Overjoyed.)* Gilbert's got one like that, because he showed me when he was sharpening it on a strop, he's got a razor with a black handle, Gilbert's got one!

SHE: We'll buy one tomorrow.

HE: *(Confused.)* Not tomorrow…

•SHE: Tomorrow. I'll go shopping and I'll buy the razor. When you've got up and had your breakfast, then you can have a shave right away.

HE: You'd better not go to that little shop for the razor.

SHE: Why not?

HE: Because there aren't any razors in that little shop…

SHE: I saw them on display today…

HE: There are no razors in the shop. You'd better buy it in another shop. In that big shop next to the station, where you always buy me my soldiers…

SHE: All right, but I still have to go to Mr Hanssen's shop to collect the milk-can…

HE: I'll get you a new can… 'Cause… 'Cause that shop's not there anymore. *(Rapidly.)* I mean, it's still there, but there aren't any razors and your milk-can's not there either 'cause the shop is burned down and everything smells in there now and don't go there anymore, don't go, because it smells awful there…

SHE: It burned down…

HE: It burned down a lot…

SHE hides her face in her hands.

HE: But don't worry, don't worry, you can buy me a razor in that shop by the station… And will you buy me some more soldiers? But make sure they're all on horseback and buy me some cannons, and an orchestra… Don't worry…

SHE: Did you go to Mr Hanssen's shop today?

HE: No, I didn't. I only stood on the other side of the street, with the banner that Gilbert gave me, and I shouted…

SHE: What did you shout?

HE: The same as everyone else…

SHE: And what was everyone else shouting?

HE: *(Shrugs.)* You know, 'Phew!' *(Holds his nose.)* 'Phew!' You know... *(Rapidly.)* 'Cause when we were walking along the street everyone was going: Aaaaaa!!! And they ran up to that shop and Gilbert took this truncheon like this *(Shows her.)* and smashed the window and then... and then, when the old man ran out of the shop with this knife – thiiiiis big it was – then all the people with the torches... But I stayed on the other side of the street, on the sidewalk, right up against the wall – with this banner that Gilbert gave me.

SHE: What happened to old Mr Hanssen?

HE: Nothing. *(Rapidly.)* But when everyone ran out of the shop, and when Mr Hanssen was kneeling in front of Gilbert and it was already burning, then his daughter ran out of the shop and hurled herself at Gilbert... *(Incredulously.)* At Gilbert... And she started to hit him... *(Fiercely.)* And Gilbert grabbed her by her curly mop *(Shows her.)* and yelled: 'You whooooooore!' *(More and more fiercely.)* And then he kicked her stupid curly-haired head...

SHE: *(Very quietly.)* What are you saying...?

HE: *(More and more excited, unfurls the banner, stands feet astride in front of her and yells, chanting.)* Filthy scum!!! Filthy scum!!!

SHE: *(Stares at him absently.)* What did you say?

HE: *(Sits down at the table, moves the plate away.)* You can always tell filthy scum... *(Rapidly.)* Gilbert says he can tell a filthy scum a mile off, by their smell. *(Fiercely.)* Dirty scum. *(Spits.)* Pta!

SHE: Don't spit on the floor.

HE: *(Slowly, cautiously.)* Why's that?

SHE: Because I spent the whole morning cleaning it... You've already scuffed it...

HE: *(Suddenly gets up from the table and stamping loudly starts to march round the table.)* Tram-ta-ta-ta-dam, tram-ta-ta-dam!!! That's how we marched, see? And I was nearly the first in the square! They came in on foot, on bicycles, in big cars. Tram-da-da-dram! Because I can do everything now. *(Stands up.)* You know? Gilbert told me to learn it all, you know? He gave me this book with pictures where everything's drawn for me, everything. And I learned everything. Don't you believe me? Look. This is 'Attention!' *(Stands at attention.)* You have to stand straight, your tummy tucked in, feet slightly bent out, palms along the seams of your trousers, head slightly raised. And 'at ease' is like this. *(Stands at ease.)* Your left foot to one side. You see how easy it is. I've learned everything: Attention! *(Stands at attention.)* At ease! *(Stands.)* See how easy it is? You try it… It's easy… Attention! At ease!

SHE: *(Smiles.)* No… I don't…

HE: But I'm telling you, easy-peasy. Go on, try.

SHE: *(Laughs.)* Leave off…

HE: *(Animated, excited, vehemently.)* 'Cause it's not all that easy. Not at all. Gilbert said you have to spend your whole life learning it. That's what he said. Your whole life. *(More slowly, cautiously.)* Some filthy old scum can't learn it. *(More rapidly.)* That's what Gilbert said. But I learnt it all very quickly, you know? Very quickly. Gilbert said: 'That's clever, that's clever…' And you know what this is: 'In two rows in front of me fall in'? Of course you don't. 'Cause it's hard… Watch. Go on, watch me! They're all walking about, walking about, you know, those who have all come to the square, and then you stand, stand at attention and you shout: 'Attention!' And then they all stand still ever so quietly, and they look, and you shout: 'In two rows in front of me – fall in!' And then they arrange themselves, ever so quickly, in two rows. See? Can you do it? No. 'Cause it's hard. And then, when they're standing like that, they have to get into fours, and then march. And then you have to shout… *(Thinks hard.)* 'By the left, quick march.' And they march, and they've got torches and banners, like this one that Gilbert gave me, 'cause Gilbert gave me this banner… Could you do that? Never in your life. Never in your life… You'll never do that… 'Cause it's hard…

SHE: *(Collects the bowls from the table, takes them to the kitchen area, he watches her every move.)* Would you like some dessert? There's some cream and some strawberries.

HE: You could never do anything like that.

SHE: *(Cautiously, kindly.)* Because only men can do it, women can't…

HE: Filthy scum can't do it, either… *(Rapidly.)* But you could do it. You could learn to do it…

SHE: *(Shakes her head and smiles.)* I couldn't…

HE: *(Slowly.)* If you wanted to, you could learn… *(Even more slowly.)* You must learn…

SHE: *(Very cautiously.)* I must learn? Why?

HE: 'Cause Gilbert tells everyone that you're…

SHE: What does Gilbert say about me?

HE: *(Thinks hard.)* That you're… *(Explodes.)* That you could learn, too, if you wanted to.

SHE: That's what Gilbert says…

HE: You must learn. I'll teach you, 'cause I've learned…

SHE: And what am I to do?

HE: You know, everything… *(Very rapidly.)* 'Cause when they go to camp then they sleep in tents there and they have watches and they shoot, and Gilbert's even used a machine gun, and they have duties, and when they went to a real military camp to an airport they even went into a plane, and Gilbert even flew in a plane, and when this filthy scum ran away from the farmer they organised a hunt for him and when they caught him in a hay loft they set fire to him, to this filthy scum, and he was running away across a field so Gilbert told them to shoot him in the legs and when he fell then Gilbert lit his cigar from him, from this filthy scum, a cigar, and others lit up their cigarettes from him 'cause only Gilbert smokes cigars, and one officer there gave Gilbert… *(Very slowly.)* Gilbert said that I would go to camp one day too…

She remains silent.

HE: Gilbert said that the most important thing is order, there's got to be order everywhere, 'cause that's the most important thing…

SHE: Yes, that is the most important thing… I think I'll lie down, I'm very tired. And I have to get up again tomorrow…

HE: You can't go to sleep. You've got to learn… It's easy. I'll teach you everything… *(Goes up to her, takes her hand.)*

SHE: That hurts…

HE: I'll teach you everything…

SHE: That hurts a lot… Let go, please…

HE: *(Loudly, straight in her face.)* Attention!!! Just look at the way you're standing!

SHE: Please…

HE: Attention!!! *(Arranges her body.)* Legs together, hands, feet pointing out. Right, now you look like a human being. Again. Attention!!! And now, at ease. Go on, at ease!!! What are you doing – dancing? At ease! Move your left foot out… *(Roars.)* Think, woman, what are you doing? *(Rapidly.)* Attention! At ease! Right! Attention! At ease!

She obeys all the instructions clumsily.

HE: And now… Drop!!!

SHE: *(Frightened now.)* What do you mean…?

HE: Ah, you don't understand… I'll show you how to do it. Only watch carefully… *(To himself.)* Drop! *(Drops to the floor.)* Did you see it? *(Gets up.)* Now you. Drop!

She kneels down on the floor clumsily.

HE: Not like that! Weren't you watching? Drop! *(He grabs the back of her neck and throws her to the ground.)* Do it again.

She gets up and falls down, clumsily.

HE: And again! On your feet! Drop! On your feet! Drop! On your feet!

She stands, breathing heavily.

HE: You see… Have a rest, go on, rest… And now something even harder. Have you had a rest? Right. Drop!

She drops to the floor efficiently.

HE: *(Walking round her.)* Good, good… Now you have to crawl. Go on, crawl, crawl… *(Squats down next to her and pulls alternately an arm and a leg.)* Arm – leg – arm – leg – arm – leg…

She freezes and her body is wracked by a sob.

HE: Are you tired? That's good. You have to get tired…

SHE: *(She stands up slowly, smiles entreatingly.)* Ooph, that's enough, I think I've learned it now…

HE: *(Confused, threateningly.)* There was no order to get up…

SHE: We'll have a break…

HE: *(More loudly.)* There was no order to get up!

SHE: I'll just catch my breath…

HE: Lie down! You're to lie down!! There was no order to get up! Drop!!! *(Presses her down on the floor.)* Drop and crawl!!! You have to learn! Right, one-two-one-two… *(Jostles her.)*

SHE: *(Breaking away, pleading.)* Leave me alone…

HE: *(Forces her to move.)* One-two-one-two…

SHE: *(More forceful.)* Leave me alone…

HE: You have to do it evenly. One-two-one-two…

SHE: *(Hysterically, breaking away.)* Leave me alone, you simpleton!!!

He freezes and gets up very slowly.

SHE: *(Gets to her knees, quietly, more to herself.)* God, I didn't mean…

HE: I wanted to teach you, to teach you… But you don't want to learn! Not at all!

She tries to get up, he pushes her and lays her down on the floor.

HE: And don't you get up! Just don't dare to get up!

He becomes threatening, she senses it and freezes as she lies there.

HE: Herr Jesus!!! Herr Jesus!!! *(Jostles her.)* You don't understand anything!!!… And now get up, you! Come on!… *(Picks her up clumsily.)* Get up! Stand 'at attention', 'at attention'! *(Puts her body into position.)* What's this, then? What's this?… *(He looks round the kitchen, as if losing the thread.)* What are you standing there like that for? Get on with your work! You have to work very hard! You've got to do a lot of work!

SHE: *(Quietly.)* What do I have to do?

HE: *(Looks for a long time, explodes.)* You must clear up! You must clean this place up!

SHE: I do clean this…

HE: *(Strongly.)* And I declare that there is disorder here! Disorder! *(Walks around her.)* Things smell bad here, smell – bad. *(Solemnly.)* Things can't go on like this, can't go on…

She is expecting the worst.

HE: You must have some training. You must learn everything. Right, don't worry, you must have some training.

SHE: *(She tries not to become panic-stricken as hard as she can.)* What are we going to do?

HE: Right, right, get packed… But you don't have a rucksack or anything… Do you have a rucksack?

SHE: No…

HE: Never mind, but it's veeeeery bad. Take that… *(He hands her the shopping bag taken off the hook on the door.)* This'll be your rucksack… Right, put something in it, put something… And you must have a belt… *(Ties a piece of string round her waist.)* And a hat… *(Puts her hat on, is pleased.)* There, see? And now we'll march, right… *(Drags her round the stage.)* One-two-one-two-one-two-one-two… And now on your own: one-two-one-two-one-two-one-two… You must lift your feet up higher, come on!

She marches.

HE: *(Watches and conducts with his arms.)* Yes! One-two-one-two-one-two-one-two… Attention!

She stands at attention.

HE: Good, see, you're in training. Is it nice doing training? *(Rapidly.)* And now you're going to sleep in a tent… Well, under the table, pretend, under the table, just pretending…

She tries to get under the table.

HE: You, wait, wait… *(Tears the oil-cloth table cover off, lays it out under the table, arranges chairs round the table, places various things under the table, like the alarm clock, mugs, table-cloths, coats taken off the hooks in the door.)* Right, see? Here's your tent… Get in there, get in…

She hurries under the table.

HE: Right, lie down, lie down… cover yourself, go on… It's comfortable, isn't it? Now sleep, go on, sleep… Right… *(Presses her head down against the floor.)* Sleep, go on, sleep….

She freezes.

HE: Are you asleep?

SHE: *(Very quietly.)* Yes…

HE: That's good. Because it's night already, it's night… *(Stands, looking ahead, glancing again and again under the table.)* Now!!! Now!!! It's morning! Stop sleeping! Reveille! *(Pretends he's playing a trumpet.)* Ta-tra-ta-dam-tatadram! Quick! Quick! *(Drags her out from under the table.)* You must get up quickly! Get up quickly! Now it's exercises! Quick! You must run! You must run! Right…

She runs round the table.

HE: … Now it's squats… One-two-one-two-one-two… Now press-ups… Right, lie down, come on, press-ups…

Very tired, her breath rasping, she tries to follow his instructions as precisely as she can.

HE: See? See?… and now you have to wash quickly… *(Drags her to the wash-basin.)* Wash now, come on…

She splashes water on herself: her hair, her clothes are wet.

HE: Wait, I'll wash, too… *(Puts his head in the wash-basin.)* Isn't this great?… Isn't it great to have a splash in the morning? *(Jostles her brutally.)* Now you must clear the tent away quickly… Come on, one-two… *(Pushes her under the table.)* Clear up, clear up…

Haplessly, she tries to arrange the things under the table.

HE: Quickly, clear up quickly… *(Drags her out from under the table, pushes her away, puts his head under the table.)* And who sleeps here?

She looks at him.

HE: *(Roars.)* Who sleeps here!!!

SHE: I do…

HE: *(Through clenched teeth.)* Why – you –you… *(Throws all the things from under the table all around the kitchen.)* Filth, stench, dirt!… You must clean all this up quickly! Quickly, you must clean it all up! *(Jostles her and forces her to collect the things.)* Tidy it, tidy it…

She tries to tidy things.

HE: Have you finished? You, get out from there… *(Pulls her out from under the table, puts his head under the table.)* Who sleeps here?

SHE: *(Crying softly.)* I do…

HE: *(Mumbles furiously, dives under the table, throws the things around the kitchen, knocks the table over with his back, knocks the chairs over.)* Tidy it up!!! *(Jostles her.)* Tidy it!

She collects the scattered things, picks up the table and chair and very carefully arranges things under the table. He gets under the table and pokes his head out, looking at her. She stands.

HE: Who sleeps here?

SHE: *(Crying.)* I do…

HE: *(Throws the things round the kitchen even more violently, makes a point of knocking over the table and chairs, punches her arm with his fist.)* What-do-you-think-you-are-do-ing? What? Learn – you – learn – you – sad – empty – head – you… *(Grabs her head with his two hands and squeezes it very tightly.)* Your head is empty… There, hear how hollow it is? *(Hits her head with his fist.)* Dum-dum-dum… dum-dum-dum…

She cries with pain and terror.

HE: *(Hands on hips.)* And what am I going to do with you? And what am I going to do with you? *(Different tone.)* What an unlucky chap he is having to be with such an empty head, such an empty head…

She tries to cuddle up to him.

HE: I am very, very unlucky that you're so… That you've got sawdust in your head. You poor, poor head… Do you know what they always say in Mr Hanssen's shop? *(Different tone.)* 'Wasted life, a wasted life with him… *(Corrects himself.)* … with her, with that unfortunate girl… The patience of a saint' is what they say… *(Rapidly.)* But I always remember what I have to buy… only your writing is always so unclear, you write so fast… And you never give me any small change, always paper notes… *(Imitates her.)* Five crowns, I'm giving you a whole five crowns… But now I've learnt everything…

SHE: Yes, I know that…

HE: But you know nothing at all, nothing…

SHE: You'll have to teach me, please…

HE: I want to!!! *(Kicks a chair.)* But you don't remember anything! *(Kicks a chair.)* Nothing at all!

SHE: *(Glances at the door, edges closer and closer to it.)* I'm such a stupid noggin… Teach me, please…

HE: *(Standing by the window.)* You must try very hard, very hard… And remember everything… So that you can give the right answers when we go *there* again…

She hurls herself at the door, opens it, he reaches her at lightning speed, they wrestle and jostle in the doorway. From beyond the window the growing roar of the crowds on the panes of the opened wings of the window, the red glimmer of the torches burning in the crowds. He drags her away from the door and throws her to the floor.

HE: *(Calmly.)* … And you always have to reply nicely when we go *there* again… *(In her voice.)* So I don't have to be ashamed of you… You'll wear that new suit of yours, that shirt, a tie and we'll comb your hair to one side, we'll comb it to one side, and we'll go back *there* again and you must reply very nicely and show and solve all the puzzles and know all the riddles, you know? And you must listen to that man and think and think – so they don't trick you – and say nothing at all about – *(Wags a finger.)* You know what… You know what… You… *(Goes up to her, and pulls her hair with all his might, knocks her down.)*

She struggles, gets away. He sits down on her, legs apart, and starts to choke her clumsily.

SHE: *(Struggling.)* Let go… let go…

HE: You must… *(Chokes her.)* You must learn…

SHE: *(Tearing herself away, catching her breath.)* You are clever! You are very clever!!! Do you hear me? Very, very clever!!! *(Dissolves in hysterical sobbing.)*

HE: *(Releases her and stands up slowly as if nothing has happened, slowly picks up the table, chairs, tidies, takes no notice of her, goes up to the dresser and turns on the radio. Rousing military marches on the radio.)* I am clever… *(Looks at her.)* And I know that you'll never learn anything at all… *(Approaches her.)*

SHE: *(Sitting on the floor, edges away.)* I will learn, you'll see…

HE: Then I have to ask you a question, a question I have to ask you… 'Cause you have to know how to answer questions…

SHE: You ask, and I'll answer…

HE: I'll do the asking… I'll ask… *(Stands in front of her.)*

SHE: May I stand up…?

HE: *(Quickly.)* You have to sit here, you have to sit…

She tries to smile expectantly.

HE: It's going to be a hard question, a hard question it's going to be…

SHE: I know. Very hard…

HE: *(Different voice.)* Tell me, boy… What do you see in this office…?

SHE: *(Kindly.)* In the kitchen?

HE: *(Hurls himself at her, roars.)* I know!!! I know it's a kitchen!!! *(Calmly, slowly.)* I just said that… I'll ask you a different question, very hard, hard…

SHE: You do ask very hard questions.

HE: Right, see… *(Different voice.)* Tell me, my boy… Tell me, my boy… *(Very rapidly.)* What do people do in the winter?

SHE: *(Gets into the part.)* In the winter, when the snow has fallen…

HE: *(Interrupts her, rapidly.)* No! Me! Me! *(Puts his hand up like a schoolboy.)* In the winter – and snow – all white – and hands are red, and the balls are all wet and we throw them *(Shows how.)* and carrying the coal and you bring the tree in and coloured balls and it's dark very quickly… *(More slowly.)* and I'm alone, and alone, 'cause you're at that stupid work and I go down to the main door and I wait and I wait for you 'cause I don't want to be alone here any more and I wait for you at the stop and there's snow and I wait and I wait and it's dark… *(Briskly.)* See? I know what you do in the winter.

SHE: That's very good.

HE: 'Cause that was a hard question, it was hard…

SHE: Very hard…

HE: *(Different voice.)* And now tell me, my boy… Just tell me, my boy… *(Thinks and searches.)*

SHE: *(Kindly.)* Go on… *(Wants to prompt him.)* Go on…

HE: *(Increasingly uncertain.)* Tell me…

SHE: *(Kindly, quickly.)* What did you dream today?

HE: *(In a flash terror, fear cross his face, he hurls himself at her and cuddles her convulsively, puts his arms round her, wants to hide.)* No… I don't want to… no more… don't… no…

SHE: *(Hugs him.)* Hush… Hush… *(Strokes him, kisses his head.)* There, there, hush now, hush…

He calms down gradually, catches his breath.

SHE: Hush now…

HE: *(Moves away from her.)* Why did you ask me that?

SHE: *(Stroking him.)* Ask you what?

HE: *(Slowly, absently.)* You know I'm not supposed to be asked a question like that. Never, you know that.

SHE: It's all right now…

HE: *(Pushes her away violently.)* You asked me that on purpose! So I would… Again… So I would… *(Very seriously.)* You're never to ask me that again, never again ask me that…

SHE: *(Shakes her head.)* Turn the radio down…

He goes up to the dresser, turns the volume of the radio right up, the radio roars out a military march. Looking at her, he starts to march on the spot: he blows a trumpet, stamps, takes two saucepan lids from the kitchen and bangs them hard and rhythmically.

SHE: Stop that!!! Calm down, will you!!! *(Runs up to him, snatches the lids from him and turns the radio off. Outside the window, the sounds of the crowds grow more and more threatening.)* God, I can't get a moment's peace with you!

HE: *(Confused.)* We're going to… Now, we're going to…

SHE: Oh, for goodness sake, give me some peace, man!

He switches on the radio and, watching her, looks for another station. The sounds of a moody, emotional waltz. She shakes her head resignedly.

HE: You must dance… You must dance… *(Tries to dance with her.)*

SHE: *(Irritated.)* Helver! Let me go!

HE: *(Pulls her powerfully towards him.)* You like to dance, you always said you like to dance…

SHE: Yes, I did, I did.

HE: Right, we'll dance.

They start to dance clumsily.

SHE: Oh, I've danced my feet off, danced them off…

Concentrating hard, he tries to catch the rhythm.

SHE: Don't jerk me about like that, it's a waltz… Feel the rhythm… Come on, left foot, right foot… Oh, come on! *(She lets go of him and dances a polka perfectly on her own, losing herself in the dance.)*

He turns the radio's volume up and twitches on the spot. The song finishes.

SHE: *(Dances for another moment then collapses onto a chair.)* I've danced myself out, I've danced myself out…

HE: Didn't you dance, then?

SHE: *(Waves her hand dismissively; a different song comes from the radio: a slow, emotional waltz.)* Turn that off…

HE: No, I won't.

SHE: Turn it off now! *(Covers her ears with her hands.)*

HE: *(Slowly.)* I know why you don't want to listen to that…

SHE: What do you know about anything…

HE: 'Cause you always cry when that lady *(points to the radio)* sings… I know why…

SHE: Leave me alone…

HE: I know…

SHE: *(Angry.)* What do you know?

HE: 'Cause when you got that from Santa Claus under the Christmas tree… When the pastor came to us that Christmas, 'cause the pastor came to us at Christmas… That's when he brought this packet for you from Santa

Claus and there was a gramophone record there in this box and on this box there was a picture of this lady that's singing now…

SHE: So?

HE: That's when the pastor told you that it was your favourite record and song and that you danced it beautifully at your… wedding…

She is very wary.

HE: And I know what a wedding is…

SHE: How do you know what the pastor said?

HE: Because I hear everything… and when I close my eyes very, very tight, then I can hear everything far, far away… *(Slowly.)* 'Cause you weddinged this man …

SHE: *(Sharply.)* Helver, stop that! *(More gently.)* The right word is married.

HE: Because you weddinged…

SHE: What are you saying…

HE: I know what that man looks like…

SHE: Helver…

HE: He has a beard and whiskers… *(Shows her.)* Oh, and he has this ribbon tied here like this… And here, on the lapel, he has this big white flower, a big white flower he has… And you have a white dress, a big one, and this handkerchief on your head where you can see your face, and flowers on your head and flowers in your hands… And you're standing there together and your heads are touching. And you're looking at him like this, and he's looking at you and you're smiling…

SHE: *(Gets to her feet violently, runs out into the room, the sound of drawers being looked through can be heard. Runs into the kitchen in a fury.)* Where is my little box?! There are very important things in it! Where is my little box!!!

HE: I didn't take your little box, I only took the box and I keep my soldiers in it…

SHE: How dare you grub around in my things!!!... Give it back!!! Do you hear me, you idiot? Give it back!!! *(Attacks him with her fists.)* You apeman! Give it back! Where is it?!

HE: *(Slowly.)* My soldiers are in it... 'Cause you buy me a lot of soldiers.

SHE: *(Shrieks.)* Where is it?!!

HE: My soldiers are in it...

SHE: *(Gets up, searches the kitchen, runs out into the room, returns.)* Where are my things, you!

HE: *(Frightened.)* They're here, under the table... *(He points to the wall-side table.)*

SHE: *(Under the table she finds a large chocolate box, opens it, furious, spills a pile of toy soldiers onto the table, hurls the box into the corner.)* Where are the things that were in here? What have you done with them? *(Shakes him.)* Well?

He lowers his head.

SHE: You've thrown them away?!!! You've thrown them away!!!? Have you? I see... You've thrown them away... You miserable apeman. *(Imitates an ape, mocking him – then with rage.)* I'm through with this! You hear me? I'm through with it. God... I must have been more stupid even than you... All those years with such a... Yuk!!! Oh, no, Master Helver... Oh, no... *(Leaps over to the dresser and pulls a large envelope with seals on it out, thrusts it under his nose.)* Do you know what this is?! Do you?!

HE: No.

SHE: *(Sadistically.)* A summons from the clinic to the admissions committee... Brand new... The postman brought it today... For tomorrow morning, do you hear? Tomorrow morning we're going to the clinic to the doctor for a little talk in his surgery... I'll pack your shitty soldiers for you, your toys and berets and we'll march over there. And the doctor will ask you: 'Tell me, my boy... Tell me, my boy... what do you see in this office!' And you'll shit yourself with fear because there's nothing in this great, empty drum of yours… *(Hits him on the head.)* Nothing, nothing at all! And then the attendants will come for you, take you and put you into a great room where there are already fifty dummies like you and you'll play with them with your shitty soldiers… And in the night…

HE: *(Curls up in fear.)* Don't talk like that… You weren't going to talk like that…

SHE: *(Overrides him.)* And in the night they turn the lights out… It's very, very dark… Whooo-hooo-hooo… And when you close your eyes… Then… Worms crawl out of your head…

HE: *(Sticks his fingers into his ears.)* I can't hear anything… I can't hear anything…

SHE: And if someone's afraid or shits themselves with fear then they pin him down with belts and make injections into those empty sconces… And if someone can't solve riddles then they put wires onto his head and do this to him with electric currents… *(Twitches.)* That's what they do…

HE: And where will you be then?

SHE: I'm going to leave you there!

HE: But you'll go with me into the office, won't you, when that doctor asks me?

SHE: *(Curtly.)* No.

HE: But where will you be?

SHE: I'll go away. I've had enough! You hear me? Enough!… Anyway, they'll take you out of the clinic right away and that'll be the end of you. Kaput. You hear me? Kaput! Kaput with you!

HE: *(Stands up and pulls out from under the dresser a pile of photographs, letters tied with a ribbon, slowly lays them before her.)* I didn't throw them away. I only took the little box… for my soldiers, 'cause I have a lot of soldiers now… I have a lot of soldiers from you… And I only hid them there…

(Points to the dresser.), I only hid those pictures and papers there so they wouldn't get lost…

She stares dumbfounded at the letters and photographs lying before her.

HE: *(Sits down opposite her and starts to stand the soldiers up on the table, pointing to a photograph with his finger.)* That's the man you weddinged…

SHE: *(Wiping her eyes.)* Yes… That is the man…

HE: Were you both… in love…?

SHE: Yes, very much indeed.

HE: And did he say to you: 'Will you wedding with me?'

SHE: *(Emotionally.)* No… he asked me if I'd do him the honour of being his wife.

HE: He said it nicely, that man…

She restrains her tears.

HE: And then what? You cried and you laughed… That's what they call… being… happy… and also… and also… de-light-ed… Is it?

SHE: It is. I was very happy…

HE: And… In love.

SHE: Yes… Very much in love.

HE: In love… that means you cried and you laughed and you cried and your eyes were merry and not sad, like they always…

She fights against the tears.

HE: So why are you here with Helver and not with this man and merry? People who wedding live together, they live together… Did we wedding?

She starts to cry.

HE: And they have babies… Did you have… *(bashfully)* a baby…?

SHE: *(A dry, broken crying, almost a whimpering.)* Yes... I did... I have... I did have a baby...

HE: A boy or a girl?

SHE: A girl... *(Cries.)* A little girl...

HE: Is she pretty?

She cries. Something inside her is breaking.

HE: And where is she now, now where is she, your little girl...?

SHE: *(Cries, sobs.)* I... I... We... This man and I... My husband and I had a baby... a little girl, very little... We were very much in love, you know? We had a house, a little garden... A little girl was born... and I... and I... when she was born *(sobs)* she was... she was very, very ill. *(Cries, weeps.)* She was like a little monkey, you know? *(Sobs.)* Like a little monkey...

HE: *(Interested.)* A little animal?

SHE: No... She was just very ill... And I... *(Explodes.)* I didn't want her... *(Through the tears.)* I mean, I wanted her... but I just couldn't... Everything before that was so beautiful. Our house and everything... And she was so, she was so... *(Sobs.)* That man, you know, my husband... Everything changed right away when I gave birth to her... He no longer smiled, he sat in the doorway, looked out at the garden and smoked cigarettes, lighting them from each other, you know? And I held her for days on end, in my arms, I cuddled her, kissed her, I wanted to calm her somehow, but she screamed without stopping; night and day, day and night, she screamed so terribly... She screamed so terribly for a whole month... And I said to my husband: 'Say something to her *(cries)*, pick her up, *(sobs)* smile at our baby.' And he'd get up, wouldn't even look at her and he'd leave the house. Once, when my husband fell asleep in the armchair after work and suddenly, quite suddenly, she stopped screaming, I covered her mouth with a napkin, because her face was so, you know... She was very very ill... and I placed her very gently on my husband's knees... *(Rapidly.)* He jumped to his feet... she fell… 'What are you doing?' I cried out… And he ran out of the house shouting: 'That is not my child!' *(Sobs.)* I waited up for him all night… And in the morning I took her to the institution.

HE: To a hospital?

SHE: Yes… No… to this institution… to a hospital, but a different kind. I took her there before five in the morning. I laid her down in front of the gates and I ran away… I ran away! *(Cries.)* And when I returned home my husband was already waiting for me… With flowers, and with this small, wooden clown, you know, that when you pull its string it moves its arms and legs… And he said that he begs me to forgive him, that he's sorry, that he thought it all through and come to understand that the baby – that she was a baby… and that everyone has the right to live… he smiled, and he cried, and he hugged me… He said he'd spent the whole night at the pastor's house, that our pastor had explained everything to him, that it was an important conversation in his life, in our life… He said there were many families which have… You know, have a different kind of child… and that they love them even more… He said… he said… that now we would love her very much, our little monkey… *(Cries, wails.)* He hugged me, kissed me and cried so very much… And then he cuddled me so long and so hard and then he said: 'And now let's go to our darling little monkey…' *(Sobs.)* And he pulled towards our baby's room… I stood rooted to the spot, I wanted to die, you know, to die… I tore myself away from his beloved embrace and ran to that institution… I don't even remember the way there… only the great, iron gate to the institution… The locked gate… And our little daughter wasn't there any more… our darling little monkey… I stood outside the gate… a crowd of workers coming out of the night shift in the factory kept jostling me… and I knew that that was the end, the end of everything… Nobody wanted to talk to me in the institution… They looked at me so strangely, and told me to get out, get out! But I knew, I felt that my little monkey was there… I started to shout, to beat those terrible doctors, sisters with evil eyes and… they called the police. They took me to the institution director's office and there… there I had to sign this paper that I… that I would never look for her… When I told my husband what had happened… *(Sobs.)* He wouldn't let me into the house… He hit me with all his strength and shouted that I was dead, that to him I was dead for ever… *(Explodes.)* How I searched for her afterwards! I searched everywhere! Years on end… I knew that when I found her we would go together to him, to that man, to my husband and… and he… *(sobs)* would hug us so tightly… hug us so tightly… *(Sobs.)*

HE: And did you find your little monkey?

SHE: No… No, I didn't… *(Strongly.)* But God Almighty is my witness that I wanted to… I would give everything just to look once at that strange darling little face… Later… when I'd been everywhere… Then finally in this great, old institution at the other end of the country… This very grey-haired doctor told me that there was no longer any need to search… 'Cause she wasn't… she wasn't on this earth any more… He said that they're not needed, that nobody wants people like her and only the good Lord God hugs them more closely than he does the others, the more ordinary ones… And that's when I really did die, you know?

HE: But you're alive…

SHE: I walked out of that institution along this long, cobbled avenue and every step seemed to be my last… and then… *(Smiles.)* I met you, Helver… You were sitting in these funny pyjamas with blue stripes on an old, wrought-iron bench under a tree in this avenue. You were looking straight ahead, swinging your legs, and you were smiling so strangely, so contentedly… Just straight ahead… We started to talk, remember?

HE: No…

SHE: You asked me if I was your mother…

HE: You're not my mother…

SHE: But I noticed in your eyes, in your smile, a hope, the hope that all this would change… that maybe in this way… *(Dry sobbing.)*

HE: And then later you took me away… We went to the station hand in hand… And there were so many people… And we travelled and travelled by train… And you bought me this coloured water to drink and later, when we got off… In that shop next to the station… You know, here, we'd arrived here… You bought me some soldiers… But that was long ago, 'cause I only had two soldiers then… *(Picks them off the table.)* This one and this one… 'Cause now I have all these… *(Proudly he shows the pile on the table.)*

SHE: That old doctor in the institution agreed. They gave me you. They summoned some committee and after a week we were here… And that's how we live, you know… Only we have to go to our clinic every three months and we must reply to questions and riddles… so they won't take you away from me… But when we go tomorrow, because we'll go together, everything will be fine…

HE: But will you go with me?

SHE: Of course I will and I'll go inside with you and I'll hold your hand, just the same… Remember? When I pinch you you'll answer the question with a 'No', and when I stroke you you'll reply: 'Yes'. Remember?

HE: Sure. The last time we were there my whole hand was all pinched, but the doctor said: 'Not bad at all, my dear boy, not bad at all.' But my hand was all pinched…

SHE: I'll make some supper now, I'll make some dumplings, all right? You like dumplings, with sauce and meat…

HE: Sure… But I'll roll the dumplings…

SHE: But don't nibble the pastry or you'll get stomach-ache…

The crash of breaking glass. Through the window and into the kitchen comes one stone, then another straight after, then a third; immediately after that a burning torch. Roar of the crowds beyond the window, groups of people are running along the steps of the staircase outside, banging on doors on various floors, the roars of people being dragged out of their homes.

HE and SHE stand, staring at the smashed window. She throws herself at the burning torch, stamps on it, pours water over it from the bowl. Sharp banging on their door.

They freeze for a moment. Outside the doors: shouts, screams, the sounds of people being dragged out of their homes, of beatings. She bolts the door and moves the table up against the door.

SHE: Helver... Now listen to me carefully... Come on, look at me... *(Shakes him.)* Look me straight in the eyes... You have to run a–... you must go... Go now...

HE: Go...

SHE: I'll explain everything... You'll get dressed... Come on, put your shoes on... Not those... The boots... They're very shiny...

HE: Gilbert said that an officer's boots must shine like a dog's bollocks... That's what Gilbert said...

SHE: Put your trousers on... *(She helps him dress.)* Come on, quickly now, put your trousers on... Do the belt up... Now your shirt... Wait, there's a button missing... I'll sew it on for you... *(She takes a needle and thread from the drawer in the table and, as she sews, says.)* Helver, do you know what we're going to do now?

HE: Now we're going to... We're going to...

SHE: *(Sewing.)* You'll dress... *(Bites the thread.)* Right, stand still... Put your coat on... That's it... We'll do the buttons up... Tighten the belt... Now the beret... My, that's a fine beret you have there, you look like a real soldier... Now sit down a moment and I'll pack your rucksack... *(She brings the rucksack in from the room.)*

HE: So you do have a rucksack after all...

SHE: I forgot about it... Remember, I'm packing a whole loaf of bread, some sausage, three apples... socks, these warm ones, a shirt... *(Wipes her tears.)* And here... *(she offers him some money in her outstretched hand)* here's some money...

Do you understand? This is a lot of crowns, a lot... Put it in your boot... Come on... *(She helps him take off his boot, then put it back on.)*

HE: But it's tight now...

SHE: It doesn't matter, you'll wear it in, you'll wear it in. It'll be our secret...

HE: All right, but it will be our secret, only ours...

SHE: Right, now put your beret on.

HE: I've got a badge here, a badge that Gilbert gave me...

SHE: Yes... It's a beautiful badge... Now we'll put the rucksack on... That's it... *(Helps him put the rucksack on.)* And now Helver is ready for his expedition, isn't he?

HE: I'm going for training, for training. Gilbert said I'd go for training...

SHE: You'll go on a very long expedition...

HE: What is an 'expedition'?

SHE: It's something even more than 'training', you know?

HE: Oh, I see...

SHE: Here... *(She hands him the banner.)* Take this with you and hold it up high, then no-one will... *(Stops herself crying.)*

HE: Gilbert gave me this banner, 'cause it was Gilbert gave me this banner...

SHE: Yes, yes... And now listen to me... Look into my eyes. You'll go out now and go straight to the station... You'll manage that, won't you?...

HE: Sure. The station's next to the shop with the soldiers...

SHE: Well done. There'll be a lot of people at the station, a lot. 'Cause everyone's running there now. They'll be running there, and shouting, and crying. But don't you look at all that, all right? Don't you worry about it...

HE: All right...

SHE: Outside the station there'll be trucks and soldiers and policemen and people with torches and dogs and banners…

HE: Like the one that Gilbert gave me…

SHE: Yes, all right. And when you stand outside the station, raise your banner and… *(Doesn't know what to say now.)* And…

HE: And I'll shout: 'Filthy scum, filthy scum!' And I'll do this… *(He runs his hand across his throat.)* This…

SHE: Excellent, Helver, well done! You're very clever. You'll walk past them, and if one of them stops you, you know, one of the ones with the torches or the dogs, just say… just say… That Gilbert gave you the banner…

HE: 'Cause Gilbert gave me the banner, Gilbert gave it me…

SHE: And that Gilbert ordered you to go to the station and that you have to go because Gilbert commanded it. Will you remember?

HE: Gilbert said…

SHE: Listen to me, Helver. You'll go to the ticket office, you know where that is, don't you? To this little window where a man or a woman sits, selling tickets… Do you understand?

HE: Sure…

SHE: And you'll ask for one ticket to Ellmit. Will you remember that? Ellmit, it's a small fishing village, on the sea-shore…That's where the institution is, this big…

HE: That's where we came from…

SHE: *(Overjoyed.)* That's right, that's right! *(Hugs him and kisses him.)* Here are seven crowns. The ticket costs seven crowns, five crowns in paper money *(she hands it to him)* and two coins of one crown each. *(Hands them to him.)* Here, hide it under your beret. When you get the ticket, hide that under your beret, too. Don't take your beret off… You'll wait for the train on the platform… Don't walk along the platform, just stand and wait… When the train comes… There'll be a terrible crowd on the platform, everyone will be pushing, shoving, shouting… Helver, listen! As soon as the train arrives on the platform run up to the nearest open carriage window, there's always some window ajar, and climb inside, into the carriage through the window, do you understand? Can you climb through?

HE: 'Course I will.

SHE: And sit without moving. Don't move. Do you hear me? Don't stand up for anything, don't stand up. And if you feel sleepy, then open your eyes very, very wide and tell yourself: 'I will not sleep, I will manage without. I'll manage without because I am clever'.

HE: So if you're clever you don't sleep?

SHE: *(Holding back the tears.)* Tonight, yes… Tonight clever people aren't sleeping… You'll be travelling all night in this train. When you get to this place, to Ellmit, remember – Ellmit, it will be morning. It'll be light, you know? That's the last station. The last, because everyone will be getting off, do you understand? You'll get off with them and you'll go straight from the station, straight from the station down this long, long avenue, straight as an arrow to the institution…

HE: That's where you came and you took me away, you brought me here…

SHE: Yes… *(Hugs him.)* That's right…

HE: *(Warily, hesitantly.)* Brought me home… home… you brought me home…?

SHE: *(Tears on her face.)* Home… To our… to your real home…

HE: *(Rapidly.)* Then why must I go there now?

SHE: Helver, listen to me, for God's sake! In this institution you'll say you have some very, very important news for doctor Gerdman. Repeat that!

HE: For doctor Gerdman.

SHE: That's right. For doctor Gerdman. He's this old man with a grey beard and these funny spectacles. He's a good man, very good. He'll remember you... Now listen carefully... You'll tell him, this doctor Gerdman, that Carla told you to go there. Carla. Repeat.

HE: That Carla told me to go there.

SHE: Very good...

HE: But you're Carla...

SHE: Well, yes, I am... And wait for me there, wait for me patiently. I'll come to you very soon, wait patiently. I'll come in two, three days at the outside...

HE: But where will you be?

SHE: I'll just arrange something very, very important here and I'll come to you right away, right away...

HE: Really?

SHE: Really... Now go, please... *(Pushes him towards the door.)* Go now... *(She goes up to the window, the roar of the crowds beyond it.)* Go now, I beseech you...

HE: *(Seizing the handle.)* But you will come for me?

SHE: I will. Helver, go now... *(Pushes him.)* Please...

HE: I want... I want...

SHE: *(Pushes him, listening to what is happening on the staircase.)* Helver, please, go...

HE: I want... You to smile at me like you did at that man in the picture... At that husband man... You to take my arm, to take my arm so we could be arm in arm...

She restrains a sob.

HE: So our heads could touch like with that man on the snap...

She embraces him and they stand haplessly like newlyweds posing for a photograph.

HE: 'Cause if you had here, now, a little girl... a little monkey like you told me about, then I wouldn't shout, not at her nor at you... I'd play with her... *(More rapidly.)* And I'd

teach her, teach her, 'cause I'd teach her... *(More slowly.)*
And I'd give her soldiers... and on my knees... and I'd
stroke her face...

SHE: *(Unable to control her sobbing, opens the door and tries to push
him out.)* Go, quickly... *(Cries.)* While you still can... Go...

HE: 'Cause you're not my mummy... Nor a lady like that...
A wife... But you are a bit like my mummy... a bit like
that lady... 'Cause now I laugh a bit and I cry a bit, which
means that I... very... I... that Helver...

SHE: *(Spasms.)* Go... *(Pushes him out into the corridor.)* Go...

He disappears behind the door.

SHE: Run... My darling... my dearest boy...

*His rapid footsteps can be heard, beyond the windows the roar of the
crowds, but the staircase is quiet. She listens, very afraid...*

*CARLA alone in the kitchen. Outside the windows the hum of the
crowd, shouts, sporadic, muffled gunshots, the barking of dogs. On the
staircase the noise of people running up and down, shouts, sporadic
blows and kicks against doors, door-handles are rattled. CARLA
hurriedly starts to pack; she brings a suitcase in from the room, puts
it down on the table, puts various things that are in the kitchen into
the suitcase: the alarm clock, a plate, the picture above the door,
chaotically, like a person who suddenly has to abandon her house, her
home. CARLA puts on her coat, her hat, glances out of the window –
slows down, gives up: escape is senseless. She sits down on a chair.
Suddenly, more intense shouts from the staircase, someone is being
beaten, pushed, that someone tears himself away – a sharp pounding
at the door, a fist beating against the door, a muffled cry... CARLA
freezes – another pounding at the door... CARLA mechanically,
accepting her fate, goes up to the door slowly and unbolts the door...
The door opens suddenly... At the same moment, the light goes out,
the power in the building has been switched off. In the kitchen, the
light from the swaying lamp outside comes through the window...
The explosion of a door being slammed... Darkness. A figure stands
by the door, breathing heavily. Constant sounds from the staircase
and the street: trucks approaching, shouts, dogs barking.*

SHE: *(In the darkness.)* Who is that? *(Lights a candle and raises it above her head.)*

Standing at the door is HELVER. Beaten, maltreated, his coat covered in mud, one shoe off, buttons ripped off, no beret, his head and face bloodied, no belt, in his hands a ripped rucksack and the broken staff of the banner.

SHE: Helver!

HE: And they tore my boot off when I was going up the stairs, when I was going up the stairs... And I don't have the banner... 'Cause Gilbert took it from me... Here, in our staircase he took it and broke it, 'cause I didn't want to give it him, 'cause Gilbert gave me that banner, Gilbert gave me...

SHE: Dear God, Helver! What do you look like? What happened?

HE: 'Cause when I was going to that station that you told me to go to, so when I went out into the street, right here, just by the gate... And there were so many people everywhere, so many... So I ran along the pavement, right next to the wall, along the wall to that great square where that big statue is, you know, this man sitting on a horse... *(Very quickly.)* So round this statue there were so many people, so many people and cars and with such black dogs and with torches, and with banners, like the one that Gilbert... And I held that banner so high, I held it so high and I ran to the station, to the station, I didn't even look at anyone, only ran towards the station... And then this man that has spots on his face, you know, the one that always shouted at us in the street, do you remember? That always shouted, always shouted such nasty things at us...

SHE: Helver, tell me what happened... Why didn't you run a–...

HE: And then he, the one with the spots, when he saw me, he started to shout, you know: 'Helver! Helver the dummy! Catch Helver! Catch the filthy scum!' And he jumped down from the truck and the others, I know them, they tripped me, they knocked me down, and kicked me and they wanted to take the banner that Gilbert gave me away… But I didn't let go… I held the banner high, I held it tight, and I shouted: 'Filthy scum! Filthy scum!' Just like you told me to do… So they kicked me here… *(Points to his head and face.)* But I still shouted… And they said such horrible things about you, such horrible things…

SHE: Helver, my dear, Helver…

HE: That you…

SHE: Don't say anything… Don't say anything…

HE: That you and me… That you do things with a filthy scum… That's what they said. They said, but it was them who said it: 'We'll screw you and that… of yours…' And they said this word, this word…

SHE: Helver darling…

HE: And then they grabbed me and threw me into the truck. And when they were carrying me onto the truck, then one of them who had this great hairy dog, he shouted to this dog: 'Hold the filthy scum, hold!' And this dog's name was Bamber 'cause then he said: 'Good boy, Bamber, good boy.'

SHE: Show me… Don't move… I'll have to disinfect it… God, there's a hole bitten out of here… Put your finger on it, there…

HE: And on this truck…

SHE: Helver, don't move, I have to clean it for you…

HE: And on this truck that they threw me into there were just the simpletons from our district, you know. The one who works in the laundry, the one whose head looks like a cucumber, the girl who always *(shows)* does this with her head and little Heinal who walks so stupidly and do you know who else was there? That stupid Helmut who collects waste paper in his pram and all people like that, you know *(taps his head)*. The whole truck… And they, these dummies, they laughed when they beat them, but some of them cried… But I didn't cry… And when this officer said: 'Take them to the clinic and put an end to them!' then I went like this… *(shows her)* and jumped straight off this truck, so they all fell over, and I ran and I ran… 'Cause I won't go to that clinic, 'cause you said you'd always go with me, that's what you said, 'cause you said that…

SHE: It's true, Helver. I'll go everywhere with you, everywhere…

HE: To that clinic, too?

SHE: Yes, to the clinic too.

HE: And when I was running away they pulled my beret off and that money for the ticket's not there any more, you know…

SHE: It doesn't matter, it's not important…

HE: But I have the money in the boot 'cause they tore off the other one here and now this boot is so tight… And when I was running away then in this doorway our pastor caught hold of me, you know? Our pastor was there. He was all dirty, dishevelled, his hands were bruised… So I told him that you told me to run to the station and that they caught me and that I escaped… So the pastor asked me where you were, and I told him that you're at home and that you've got to arrange so many very very important things and that in two, three days you'll come to me to that Ellmit, to Ellmit.

SHE: What else did our pastor tell you? What did he say?

HE: The pastor said that I have to run to you very fast… to run home… So I told him that you told me to go to the station and travel to Ellmit, to Ellmit. So the pastor said that now you want me to run home quickly – so I did. And they pulled that boot off on the stairs 'cause they wanted to catch me, but I kicked them away and ran upstairs… But they shouted after me, you know… When they were dragging old Mr and Mrs Wilde out of their home, and their little grandson Taddy who laughs so stupidly and only goes round and round in circles, they yelled after me: 'Go on, run away, run away home, we're coming for you, Helver, we're coming for you...' And they said such a terrible word, such a word... And then Gilbert called out...

SHE: Is Gilbert here?

HE: Sure. He's just standing there and supervising while they're dragging old Mr and Mrs Wilde and others out of their apartments, and he grabbed that little Taddy's head and banged it against the wall, against the wall. And he yelled: 'Disgusting shit! Disgusting shit!' So Gilbert called out after me: 'You're dead, filthy scum! You're dead!' I'm not a filthy scum, am I?

SHE: No, no Helver, you're not a filthy scum... What else did our pastor say to you? Try to remember... Well?...

HE: He said... he said... 'Tell Carla...'

SHE: Yes, what? What were you to tell me?

HE: Our pastor said: 'Helver, tell my dear Carla that out Lord knows what he is doing.' That's what he said.

SHE: Is that all?

HE: He also said...

SHE: What else did he say?

HE: Our pastor said: 'Pray with Carla for yourselves, for me, for everyone.' And then he said he was going back to the church 'cause the church was burning... Did you know? The church is burning and he's going to pray for us, too, for himself and for everyone... And the church is burning so there's a glow coming from it like from our factory when they open all the furnaces, this glow...

SHE: *(Approaches the window carefully.)* Yes... Our church...

HE: Now we're going to... We're going to now... I know! Now we're going to pray! And I know how to pray! I know! 'Cause you always taught me, always. You pray to those pictures you have over your bed and to those pictures that you have in that small black book... I know how to pray... *(Kneels and pulls her down to the floor, she kneels down next to him.)* This is what you do… *(Crosses himself.)* Isn't that right? You see, I did learn… And you bow your head like this… 'Now I lay me down to sleep…' What's the matter? Don't you remember? You say the prayer, you say it… 'Now I lay me down to sleep, I pray the Lord my soul to keep.' See? I did learn it. You say the prayer, you say it…

SHE: *(Gets up decisively.)* Helver! Do you know what?

HE: What?

SHE: We'll play a game now, we'll play… build-ing-blocks!

HE: How do you play that?

SHE: Come on, I'll show you. Get up. We'll put the table here, clear this up… Come on, help me… Take the suitcase into the room… I took it out because I was doing a bit of clearing… Come on, quickly…Right, the table's clear… Now some chairs… We'll light the candles, pass me the candlestick from the dresser, and light all the candles… That's right… We'll make ourselves a big mug of tea each… Oh, dear, what am I like, there's no power… We'll just pour ourselves a large mug of water with cherry juice… That's it… Right, sit down at the table, Helver… that's it… I'll sit down, too, I'll just bring some… *(She takes, out of a drawer in the dresser, three quite large medicine bottles made of brown glass, and puts them down on the table.)*

HE: But those are my pills.

SHE: That's right… But now we'll pretend they're building blocks.

HE: But they're my pills that you always buy for me at Mrs Kersten's chemist's shop. And there's a skeleton in that shop, in a cupboard… And Mrs Kersten always says: 'Swallow the pills, swallow them, Helver, or the skeleton will come for you.' Why does she say that? I mean, I do swallow the pills, I swallow them.

SHE: You swallow your pills very nicely, Helver, only sometimes you do complain…

HE: Because they stick in my throat, here… *(Shows her.)*

SHE: You swallow them very nicely, very nicely indeed. And that skeleton at the chemist's is made of cardboard, you know? It's just a model, a pretend skeleton, not real.

HE: So that skeleton won't come for me?

SHE: No… *(Verging on breaking down in tears.)* He won't come… Helver, listen. There are three bottles of pills here… I'll pour them all out… *(Pours them out onto the table.)* There, see? See how colourful they are? Look how many there are!

HE: But I know. These… *(Shows which.)* … The green ones, you always give me them in the morning – always two so that… the day is bright and good and… *(rapidly)* and I don't wave my arms about… And these… *(Looks for them on the table.)* The red ones – you always give me those after dinner so that… so that I can learn and remember and have a clever head… Oh, and these… *(Searches for them on the table.)* The white ones, you always give me those before I go to sleep so that… so that I have good dreams and I can sleep and sleep… 'Cause when you're asleep… you're asleep.

(CARLA runs her fingers through the coloured pills scattered on the oil-cloth covered table. Her face is tense, but she manages to conceal her expression with a warm smile, trying to draw HELVER into the game of 'building blocks'. Only her eyes are vacant and motionless. She's not even crying now, the tears fill her eyes of their own accord, occasionally during the game she suppresses a sob.)

SHE: Helver, now we're going to build a coloured house out of these pills. Well, how do you build a house?

HE: *(Thinks about it, moves the pills on the table.)* First… First… *(Starts to arrange them.)* Make a square… There, then the roof… But I'll make it out of the red pills… Then the chimney… And a little tree… And I'll make some windows! I'll make windows!

SHE: Helver, we forgot about your before sleeping pills. Look how late it is.

HE: Yes, it's quite late… *(Continues to play.)*

SHE: Well, swallow these two white ones… *(Gives him the pills.)* And have a sip of water. It's very cold.

HE: *(Takes the pills, concentrating on the game, puts them in his mouth and takes a sip of water.)* I'll make a sun… There… What else can I make?

SHE: What a beautiful picture you've made there… You know what? Have some more… *(She gives them to him.)* Two green, two red, and two white. Swallow them, and you won't need to swallow them tomorrow, all right?

HE: Sure… *(Still playing, he swallows the pills and sips some water.)* So what shall I make now?

SHE: Make… Make a ship. With a mast, and funnels, and the waves of the sea…

HE: *(Enthusiastically.)* Fine… *(Starts to make it.)* But you make something, too. Look how many pills there are here… What will you make?

SHE: What about a flower?

HE: Who would the flower be for?

SHE: For you, Helver…

HE: For me? *(Shrugs.)* I never had a flower, not from you, not from anyone. What use is a flower to me?

SHE: It'll be a flower just for you… *(Starts to make it.)*

HE: *(Building.)* And what's my ship going to be called?

SHE: Ships have all sorts of names…

HE: But what? But what?

SHE: Well, like towns, or important people, or just names, all sorts…

HE: But what? *(Yawns, and very, very gradually becomes sleepy.)*

SHE: Helver, what colour pills do you like most of all?

HE: I like them all… But I think the green ones most of all…

SHE: *(Through suppressed sobs.)* Know what, I bet you couldn't swallow any more pills…

HE: I could. Which ones?

SHE: *(Through sobs, despairing.)* Four green, four red, four white... Could you swallow that?

HE: Certainly. *(Picks out a handful of pills, puts them in his mouth, sips some water, yawns.)* I swallowed them. It wasn't hard. They're good. 'Cause that coloured thing on them is sweet, you know?

SHE: You like sweet things?

HE: Sure. But most of all I like it when you bake a cake or some doughnuts... *(Yawns, his eyelids start to droop slowly, his movements become ever slower.)* Or when you make little tarts with jam in the middle... I like sweet things...

SHE: *(Through broken sobbing.)* Then swallow a few more of the white ones, then some red ones, and the green ones, but keep them in your mouth a bit longer and you can tell me which are the sweetest...

HE: *(Ever more slowly, sleepily, slow, imprecise movements.)* Now I'll make myself an aeroplane... *(Starts to build, and takes the pills into his mouth, sucking them like sweets.)* They're sweet when you suck them, sure... And what are you going to make now?

SHE: What would you like?

HE: *(Building.)* Make me something... so I won't be so... you know? Such a Helver, so I won't be...

SHE: *(Through suppressed spasms.)* You're the most magnificent, good, dearest...

HE: *(Very slowly, very sincerely.)* But I'm such a... I'd like to be... so that... But I can't do that... And so my head wouldn't be so... So it wouldn't be so...

SHE: My dear, good Helver...

HE: I've swallowed a lot of these pills today... And you always said... And you always said to 'take only two, only two'... I don't think I'll make anything else now... 'cause there are only one, two, three, four, five, six pills left... See? I don't think you'll make anything, either... So shall I swallow the rest of the pills?

SHE: *(Through her sobs.)* Yes... swallow them quickly, Helver... Swallow them...

He takes them and puts them into his mouth, tries to say something, but he chokes, coughs, the pills fall out onto the table, the floor. A coughing fit. She jumps up from her chair, hurriedly collects the pills from the table and the floor and stuffs them into HELVER's mouth. He is consumed by coughing, pushes her away. She overcomes his feeble resistance, puts the pills into his mouth and pours water down his throat. He splutters, spitting the water out, slowly recovers his breath.)

HE: I've swallowed them, I've swallowed them. *(Slumps in the chair.)*

SHE: I know, I know... my darling...

HE: My tummy hurts and my head and here... See, see how fast my heart is beating... *(Puts her hand on his chest.)* Can you feel it? Like a machine-gun: tu-tu-tu-tu-tu...

SHE: Have some water, have some more water...

HE: There, next to the table leg, there are two more pills... *(Strains to look.)* Green ones, or white... they must be gold...

She picks the pills up from the floor, holds them in her hand, then throws them into the corner, hides her face in her hands and weeps convulsively.

HE: *(On the edge of unconsciousness.)* Don't you cry... Don't cry... I'll swallow those, too... I'll swallow them as I... *(Slumps over the table.)*

SHE: *(A terrifying scream.)* No!!! No!!!

HE: I think I'll go to sleep... But you'll hug me, cheek to cheek... And give me something to hold... Give me a soldier... the one on the horse... And say something to me... Say.. *(Falls heavily off his chair and onto the floor.)*

SHE: *(Kneels down next to him, jostles him violently.)* Helver!!! Helver!!! *(More quietly.)* Helver... *(Sobs.)*

HE: *(Cuddles against her with the last remnants of consciousness.)* Hug me tight... Kiss me... *(She hugs him, kisses him, her face covered in tears.)* And do this on my face... *(Takes her hand and uses it to stroke his face.)* On my face... *(Very quietly, almost silently.)* 'Cause Gilbert gave me... *(More quietly.)* Gilbert gave me... *(And more quietly still.)* Carla... *(Shallow, final breaths.)* Mummy... mummy... mum-my... mu...

SHE: *(Scream, sob, frenzy.)* Forgive me!!! Forgive me!!!... Forgive me, Lord... *(Breaks off – breath – eruption – a hysterical yelp.)* Because You alone know what You are doing!!!??? *(Sob.)* You know? What do you know? What?! *(Tries to lift HELVER's body.)* Look! Look what you've done! *(Hugs HELVER's body.)* Why!? *(From a scream to a sob.)* He knew his prayers... *(Dry spasms.)* Knew them like no-one else!... Sure! *(Jostles HELVER's body.)* Tell Him! Tell Him!... *(Sobs into whimpers.)...* I pray the Lord my soul to keep... Do you hear? Do you hear how beautifully he says his prayers? *(Sobs.)* You should have listened only to him... Only to him... *(Quietly.)* Only him...

A violent hammering at the door, kicking. CARLA knows that this is the end. Yells outside the door. Through the window, several stones are thrown into the kitchen, the sound of truck horns and dogs barking. CARLA hugs HELVER's body, strokes it, embraces it, covers it gently with his torn coat. CARLA gets up slowly. Looks at the door which seems to be about to come out of its frame. She adjusts her hair, her dress, very slowly turns towards the audience and smiles. There is in this smile, through the tears and the fear, a kind of determination, a knowledge of the end, an attempt at justification, expectation of understanding, but this smile must also protect her from sympathy, guard her against any attempt at belief in hope. CARLA takes two steps towards the audience, smiles and looks. The door flies out of its frame with a crash. CARLA stands motionless, looking at the audience. She is by now outside the world of the stage. There is only she and the audience.

Suggestive, absolutely illusory sounds of people rushing into the kitchen, sounds of beating, a scream, kicking, heavy breathing. They run down the stairs, dragging two bodies which bang against the steps of the staircase. CARLA keeps standing and smiling. Slow brightening of the house lights.

The music starts. As the lights go on we hear the swelling sound of the waltz, the same one that CARLA danced so beautifully. The music accompanies the audience as it leaves the auditorium, in the foyer, in the cloakrooms and for a long time after it has left the theatre from the outside loudspeakers, in the street.

Ralf N. Höhfeld

BUSSTOPKISSER

Translated by Vanessa Fagan

Further Copyright Information

Busstopkisser

Characters

A GIRL

A BOY
(who can only speak 160 characters at a time,
then he needs a break[1])

Location:
A bus stop, over time

---

[1]The 160 characters refer to the original maximum length of characters in a text message. The translation keeps to this technique wherever possible, resulting in deliberate, sometimes mid-word breaks as occurs in the German original. In some instances breaks after exactly 160 characters would have made the flow of speech unintelligible in English and characters had to be added. Wherever this was necessary, the translation has used the closest number of characters to 160 to still reflect the original as far as possible.

Company of Angels funded two research-and-development presentations for inclusion at Theatre Café Festival York in February 2014. Action To The Word shared their excerpt of *Busstopkisser*, going on to develop the full production for a run at Camden People's Theatre, 24th June – 6th July 2014.

The beginning of January. A bus stop. With bus shelter. It's snowing. A GIRL arrives. With a holdall. She walks into the shelter. She looks around. But it isn't entirely clear: Is she looking outside – or looking at her reflection in the glass.

GIRL: Hey, my name is Lulu.

Silence.

My name is Bella.

Silence.

I'm Emmanuelle.

Silence.

I'm Lilli.

Silence.

My name is Brigitte. Well: Brijitt.

Silence.

My name is Angelina.

Silence.

I'm Käthchen.

Silence.

My name is Summer April.

Silence.

I'm Uma.

Silence.

I'm Marlene.

Silence.

I'm Pippilotta[2].

---

[2]Pippilotta is a reference to the lead character in the popular Swedish children's book series *Pippi Longstocking* by Astrid Lindgren.

Silence.

My name is Romy.

A BOY arrives.

BOY: I'm Tom.

Silence.

GIRL: Hi Tom.

BOY: Hi…

GIRL: My name is…

BOY: Romy. I heard.

The BOY approaches the GIRL. Takes her in his arms. And kisses her.

BOY: Wow.

Silence.

BOY: Stuff like that doesn't normally happen to me.
        I mean, usually, when I meet a girl,
        it takes 18 months, as a rule, until the first time, we

Pause.

BOY: kiss.

Silence.

BOY: How about you?

Silence.

BOY: This is totally surreal, right?

Silence.

BOY: What are you up to out here? Other than kissing.

GIRL: I'm waiting for the bus.

Silence.

BOY: Where are you going? I mean, maybe we are headed
        the same way.

GIRL: To the airport.

BOY: Hm. Not my way. That means, you're going to leave me already?

Silence.

BOY: Shall I fly with you? I mean, to me it does feel a little bit like we've already been together for 18 months, know what I mean? So in that case we could easi

Pause.

BOY: ly go on holiday together…

Silence.

GIRL: I'm not going on holiday.

BOY: But?

GIRL: To school.

Silence.

BOY: Before you fly, can I… again…?

Silence.

The BOY kisses the GIRL.

BOY: Where is your school?

GIRL: In England. A public school.

BOY: Is that where you learn to kiss like that? I want to go to England, too.

Silence.

BOY: I can't afford that.

Silence.

BOY: If your parents are paying the school fees, why don't they bring you to the airport? Why don't they pay for a cab?

GIRL: They're not here. My mum is in New York, with her new boyfriend. And my dad is at an opening night, in Esslingen[3].

BOY: I'd never let my daughter fly to England on her own. And definitely not by bus.
The things that could go wrong.

Silence.

BOY: We can chat, tweet, skype. We live in the 21st century, even if you are a few hundred kilometres away.
But really you're right here in my

Pause.

BOY: arms.

Silence.

BOY: I'll miss the kissing.

Do you really have to go to school?

GIRL: Yes. But I'm gonna be back.

Silence.

GIRL: My bus.

They look at each other. The BOY kisses the GIRL.

BOY: It was nice with you. Romy.

The GIRL leaves.

BOY: Hey, can you give me your mobile number, your email address, your…

The GIRL is gone.

The BOY leaves.

---

[3]Esslingen is a small town on the edges of the former coal-mining region in West Germany with a rather limited, perhaps underwhelming, cultural scene. The reference indicates that the 'opening' is a second-rate affair, most closely similar perhaps to some neglected regional theatres in rural England – not to be confused with one of the many very vibrant, current rural / regional theatres.

2.

Half a year later.
The bus stop. The sun is shining.
The BOY arrives, with a flower in his hand. He waits.
The GIRL arrives.

BOY: Hi.

GIRL: Hi.

Silence.

BOY: Well, that's a coincidence.
         You remember? Half a year ago we met here.

Silence.

BOY: Have you just come back from England? You're on
         holidays, right?

Silence.

BOY: How about a welcome…?

Silence.

The BOY kisses the GIRL.

BOY: Here. For you.

He hands the flower to the GIRL.

GIRL: Thank you.

BOY: I thought, if your parents are away and they can't
         come to collect you, that maybe you'd be happy to
         have someone waiting here for you. Someone who
         welcomes

Pause.

BOY: you.

Silence.

BOY: Are you happy?

GIRL: Yes.

Silence.

GIRL: How did you know I was arriving today?

BOY: Ah. I've googled the English public school system
        a bit. Managed to find out holiday dates from 50
        schools and then calculated the avera

Pause.

BOY: ge for the first day of the holiday season. Then added
        a day for partying and packing and departure and
        things like that. And the result was: today. Very sim

Pause.

BOY: ple.

GIRL: I am im…

Silence.

GIRL: …pressed.

Silence.

GIRL: Sorry. I'm really sorry.

Silence.

GIRL: And I really ought to go, my mum is waiting.

BOY: Before you go…

The GIRL is ready to kiss.

BOY: No, not yet. Can I take a picture of you first?

The BOY takes a picture of the GIRL with his mobile.

BOY: Thank you. And now…

The BOY goes to kiss the GIRL.

GIRL: Out of time.

The GIRL leaves.

BOY: Hey! Romy, what's your mobile number again, your
        email…

The GIRL is gone.
The BOY looks at his mobile. Then kisses the display.
The BOY leaves.

3.

Eight weeks later.
Same place. The sun is shining.
The BOY arrives.

BOY: *(By himself.)* At English public schools the average
holiday time is eight weeks. She should…

The GIRL arrives.

GIRL: Hi.

BOY: Hi.

Silence.

BOY: Before you have to go off again, you have to give me
your mobile number and email address first of all.

Otherwise there's no kiss.

Silence.

GIRL: I'm sorry. I haven't got a mobile number or an email
address.

BOY: What?
That's impossible. You're joking!

GIRL: No.

BOY: How can you live like that?

Silence.

GIRL: Does that mean I don't get a kiss?

The BOY kisses the GIRL.

GIRL: Today is our third date.

BOY: I know.

Silence.

GIRL: I brought coffee and cookies for us.

She unpacks a flask, mugs and cookies.

BOY: And a candle for you.
Actually, it was meant for those dark autumn evenings, so that you can think about me, at candlelight. But I could just as well light

Pause.

BOY: it now.

GIRL: Yes. That would be nice.

They drink coffee and eat cookies at candlelight.

GIRL: You have to eat and drink a little faster.
I don't have all that much time.

The BOY shoves a cookie in his trouser pocket and finishes his drink quickly.

BOY: Done.
That was a nice idea of yours. With the coffee…

GIRL: Hm.

The GIRL quickly wraps up the remains.

BOY: Thank you.

GIRL: My bus.

BOY: My kiss.

The BOY kisses the GIRL.

GIRL: My candle.

The GIRL leaves.

The BOY sits down. He frowns. Gets up again. Puts his hand in his pocket. Has crumbs all over his hand. Eats them, bit by bit. At the end he licks his hand. And leaves.

4.

The beginning of October. Same place.
The BOY arrives.
He sits down. He looks around. Looks up at the sky. Looks at his watch.
The BOY leaves.

5.

Just before Christmas. Same place.
The BOY arrives. He is wearing a Santa hat.
The GIRL arrives.

BOY: Hi.

GIRL: Hi.

BOY: Long time.

GIRL: Yes.

The BOY kisses the GIRL.

Silence.

BOY: I've got something for you. For Christmas. Or for
          your birthday. But somebody who hasn't got a
          mobile number or an email address probably hasn't
          got a birthday, either, right?

Laughs.

GIRL: Yes I do.

BOY: Coming up? Or has it been and gone?

GIRL: Been and gone. 4 weeks ago.

The BOY kisses the GIRL.

BOY: All the best. Happy belated birthday.

GIRL: Thank you.

BOY: Your present.
          Don't you want to unwrap it?

The GIRL unwraps the present.

GIRL: A mobile?

BOY: No. That's just the box.

The GIRL continues to unwrap. Inside the box there is a picture frame. With a picture of the BOY and the GIRL.

BOY: Do you like it? We obviously hadn't got a picture of us together yet. So I made one up on the computer. Remember I took that photo of you here at the bus st

Pause.

BOY: op. So I photo-shopped myself in next to you. And for a backdrop I added a Cuban beach. The two of us in Cuba. Isn't that a great pres

Pause.

BOY: ent? Do you like it?

GIRL: Yes. Cuba. I've always wanted to go there.

Arm in arm they're looking at the picture.

GIRL: It looks so real.

Silence.

BOY: Hey. Are we going to go away together at some point? For real?

GIRL: And where would you want to go? Cuba?

BOY: Maybe something closer by, for a start. And cheaper.

GIRL: And?

BOY: The Lüneburger Heide[4]?

GIRL: Hm.

BOY: No. Paris.

GIRL: Oui.

---

[4]Famous large area of marshlands/moors in Northern Germany, similar to the Yorkshire Moors.

BOY: Oui?

GIRL: Oui.

BOY: Oui nice.

Silence.

GIRL: I have to go.

BOY: No.

GIRL: Yes.

BOY: No. You can stay for a bit. I'm getting live departure times for London sent to my mobile. The afternoon flight is delayed. You can

Pause.

BOY: wait out two busses.

GIRL: Really?

BOY: Yes. Quite useful, having a mobile.

Silence.

GIRL: And what do we do with that spare time?

The BOY looks at the GIRL and kisses her.

GIRL: And now what?

BOY: Erm.

GIRL: Yes?

Silence.

GIRL: Oh well.

Long silence.

GIRL: It's been nice with you.

BOY: With you, too.

GIRL: See you soon.

BOY: Yes.

GIRL: Happy Christmas.

The GIRL hands the BOY a package.
The GIRL leaves.
The BOY unwraps. And then holds a small Eiffel Tower in his hands.

6.

Beginning of January. Same place.

The BOY arrives. He's holding a rose in his hand. There are already four roses at the bus stop, all in different stages of decay. He looks. Waits. Then he takes his mobile and makes a call.

BOY: Hi Mario. – Yes, where else. – She either takes an earlier or a later flight deliberately. Or she's getting her Mum to drive her to the airport. Or her Dad. Or sh

Pause.

Boy   e takes a cab. Or walks. Or whatever. Just so she doesn't have to see me. She doesn't like me anymore. – And it was just starting to be nice and interesting. A

Pause.

BOY: nd intense and intimate. We saw each other four times. Kissed nine times. And that's supposed to have been it? Just after a year, it's

Pause.

BOY: all over already? Was I too full-on? Or too shy? Was she expecting more 'action' from me? Well, not so long ago, we had a bit of spare

Pause.

BOY: time. I'd already kissed her and then we were just sitting here. Next to each other. In silence. Without moving. I felt that prickling

Pause.

BOY: all over my hands, but… I didn't do anything,
         nothing at all. You know I'm not really the daredevil
         type, not at all, well except for that first kiss, maybe.
         Bu

Pause.

BOY: t other than that? What was I supposed to do?
         – Yes. For five days. –
         Yes, of course. A new one every day. Looks around.
         I think the bin men are on strike. – What? – You

Pause.

BOY: mean ground staff or pilots might be striking, too? –
         Hm. – What should I do? – Yes, I know! I know! I'll
         be in touch! Laters!

The BOY hangs up. Throws away the rose and runs off.
A little later the GIRL arrives. She looks around. She looks sad.
Then she notices the roses. She smiles. And collects all five roses.
The GIRL leaves.
The BOY returns. He's holding a poster under his arm. He hangs
the poster up on the bus stop: A fairly blurry picture of the GIRL,
underneath the words 'Looking for Romy!' and his mobile number.
He looks at the poster. Looks around. He notices the roses are gone. He
thinks. And grins. He looks at the poster. Looks around. Then he kisses
the poster.
And leaves.

7.

Just before Easter. Same place.
The BOY arrives. With a holdall. His phone rings.

BOY: Yes, hello? – Yes, that was me. – Yes. – You've seen
         her? Whereabouts? – On the underground. – In New
         York? – You're sitting on the subway to Coney Island.
         And she's there, too? – Yes, thanks a lot. You've been
         a great help. – Bye.

The BOY's phone rings.

BOY: Yes, hello? – Yes, that's mine. – Yes. – And where exactly? – Garmisch-Partenkirchen. Ah. – She's wearing a red winter jacket and drinking a cup of hot chocolate. –

The GIRL arrives.

BOY: Okay. Many thanks. You've been a great help.

GIRL: Hi.

BOY: Hi.

GIRL: What's up?

BOY: You're sitting in a café in Garmisch-Partenkirchen at the moment, drinking hot chocolate.

GIRL: I don't even like hot chocolate.

The BOY's phone rings.

BOY: Yes, hello? – Yes, that was me. – Where? – High Street in Leverkusen. – Yes, that's possible. – Yes, many thanks for your troubles.

GIRL: Leverkusen?

BOY: Yes, you're just entering Nanu-Nana[5].

The BOY's phone rings.

BOY: It's been going on for a few weeks. People are very helpful. And the places you've been. New York, Leverkusen, Rio. Just England, no one has ever seen you th

Pause.

BOY: ere. *(Answers the phone.)* Yes, hello? – Yes, where? – Oh yes, that's me. Many thanks for your help.

GIRL: And where am I now?

BOY: Next to me. The guy over there recognized you.

---

[5]German knick-knack / stationery shop chain similar to Paperchase in the UK.

The BOY kisses the GIRL.

Silence.

GIRL: Why are those people calling up?

The BOY points to the poster.

BOY: At the beginning of January, you weren't here
            and so I...

GIRL: No, I was here. I got your messages.

BOY: My messages?

GIRL: The ones scattered around here.

BOY: Ah, I see.

Silence.

BOY: It was our anniversary.

GIRL: I know.

BOY: And I thought...

GIRL: What?

BOY: Nothing.

The BOY kisses the GIRL.

BOY: Nice to have you back.

Silence.

BOY: Hey. I've been thinking about us. About our...
            I mean, I'm not entirely happy with the way this is
            going.

Silence.

BOY: I think we don't see each other often enough. We
            should get some more time together. Maybe 20
            minutes in one setting at some point. Or four hours
            Or maybe ev

Pause.

GIRL: en a whole weekend.

BOY: Exactly.

Silence.

GIRL: That would be nice.

BOY: Yes.

GIRL: But when?

BOY: Now.

GIRL: Now?

BOY: Yes. I've got my bag. Paris awaits.

GIRL: Paris?

BOY: Oui.

The BOY shows the GIRL the little Eiffel Tower.
Silence.

GIRL: I can't.

BOY: Yes you can.

GIRL: No. My parents are waiting for me. Both of them.
        We're celebrating Easter together.

BOY: I've reserved a table for 8pm.

GIRL: In Paris?

BOY: Yes. Chez Pauline. In the Rue Villedo. They do
        traditional haute-cuisine. I thought you'd like that.

Silence.

BOY: Our coach is leaving over there. In exactly 20
        minutes. After we get there, we'll have time to freshen
        up quickly at the hotel and to kiss. We hand over
        your dir

Pause.

BOY: ty laundry, kiss, and then we go out for a bite to eat.
          Afterwards we kiss and stroll along the boulevards.
          We look at the Seine and the Eiffel Tower, the re

Pause.

BOY: al one, and kiss. Later we'll lie in our room, listening
          to French music from the radio and kissing. Stuff like
          that. Unless you've got something better to do to

Pause.

BOY: day?

GIRL: I've never had anything better to do in my life.
          But just today, I do.

Silence.

GIRL: My mum is coming over especially from New York.
          We'll all play happy family and eat together. I'll cook,
          light candles, put some music on.

BOY: We'll be sitting at Chez Pauline's and enjoy our
          starters. The ones with those wonderful French names
          we unfortunately don't understand. And afterwards,
          we ki

Pause.

BOY: ss.

GIRL: I'll try to get my mum and dad back together again.
          Real close.

BOY: We'll be enjoying the main course, some dish with
          a wonderful French name, of which we'll be able to
          understand about thirty-five percent. And afterwards
          we'll ki

Pause.

BOY: ss.

GIRL: They'll be getting ever so close. Tonight. As close as
          possible.

BOY: This will be our night. The two of us. All by ourselves. In Paris.

GIRL: I have to go.

The GIRL leaves.

BOY: No.
       If you leave now, you never need to bother coming back.

The GIRL hesitates. And is gone.
The BOY sits down. At some point, his phone rings.

BOY: Hello? – Yes, that's mine. – Yes. – And where? – Paris.
       – Thanks a lot.

He takes the small Eiffel Tower out of his jacket pocket and looks at it.
Then he throws it away.
Some time later.
The GIRL returns. She sees the small Eiffel Tower, picks it up.

GIRL: And how about if this was our Paris?

She puts the Eiffel Tower down on top of the bus shelter.
Then the GIRL leaves.

GIRL: See, from here we have a great view of the Eiffel Tower. I'll come to Paris tonight, here. Will you be there? Will you wait for me?

BOY: Is that really you?

The BOY gets up and kisses the GIRL.
Then the GIRL leaves.

8.

Later.
The BOY takes a thick jacket out of his bag and puts it on.
Then night falls and he falls asleep.
The GIRL arrives.

GIRL: Tom?

BOY: Romy?

The BOY kisses the GIRL.

GIRL: Are you hungry? I brought German haute-cuisine.
        Chicken drumsticks. Want some?

BOY: Yes.

The GIRL spreads a blanket. Puts the food out.

BOY: Yummy. Don't you want any?

GIRL: I've already had some. At home.

BOY: How did it go?

GIRL: My parents started arguing before we even got to
        dessert. I wanted them to stop, and I started
        screaming. At the top of my voice. But they didn't
        even hear me. Not at all.

The BOY embraces the GIRL.

Silence.

BOY: You know, this is the first time you're not in transit.
        You're simply here. With me.

GIRL: Yep. In the middle of the night. In Paris.

BOY: And we have time.

GIRL: The whole night.

The BOY kisses the GIRL.

BOY: That was the fourteenth kiss I gave you.

GIRL: Your lips are all greasy. But it doesn't matter.

The BOY kisses the GIRL.

BOY: Fifteen.

The BOY and the GIRL lie there and look at the stars.
The BOY takes his mobile and headphones and looks for a radio station.
Then both listen with one ear each to French music.

BOY: French music isn't all that bad.

GIRL: Paris at night is wonderful.

BOY: Yes. And we kiss.

The BOY kisses the GIRL.

BOY: So.

GIRL: As you said.

They lie there.
And at some point fall asleep.
Later.

GIRL: Tom?

BOY: Romy?

GIRL: I've brought German haute-cuisine.

BOY: Chicken drumsticks?

GIRL: Yes.

BOY: You're not eating?

GIRL: Had some already.

BOY: They're really greasy.
        But that doesn't matter.

The BOY kisses the GIRL.

GIRL: Fifteen.

BOY: No. Seventeen.
        The night is wonderful.

GIRL: Yes.

BOY: You too.

They're listening to French music.
At some point they fall asleep.

GIRL: Tom?

BOY: Romy?

GIRL: I must have fallen asleep.

BOY: Me too.

GIRL: I had a dream.

BOY: About us?

GIRL: No. About my father and my mother.
          They're sitting in a restaurant. Greek.
          They've ordered, drank an Ouzo, and now they're
          waiting for their food. They're talking and discussing
          how to name their child, the child of whom they've
          known for the past few days that it'll be a girl.
          Lulu, says my dad. Bella, says my mum.
          Emmanuelle, says my dad. Lilli, says my mum
          Brigitte, well Brijitt, says my dad. Angelina, says
          my mum. Uma, says my mum. Marlene, says my
          mum. And then my dad says: Pippilotta. He laughs
          and finishes the conversation with that comment.
          His 'Cyprus Platter' arrives, with gyros, souvlaki and
          those meatballs filled with cheese. My mum only has
          a Greek salad. They eat in silence. I'm no longer
          important at all. I try to scream, I try to kick my mum,
          but she doesn't notice.
          Neither does my dad.
          Hold me.

The BOY embraces the GIRL.

BOY: We're here in Paris. Just the two of us.

GIRL: Yes.

BOY: Greece is far away. And your parents, too.

The BOY kisses the GIRL.

BOY: Eighteen.

They're lying there. And at some point they fall asleep.

GIRL: Tom?

The BOY doesn't react.
The GIRL gets up, packs up the blanket and food and leaves.
Later. The BOY wakes up.

BOY: Romy?

Silence.

BOY: Do you remember, the first time we met?
         That morning I shot up courage. I shot thirty guys
         in Call of Duty. That's one of those console games,
         where you're a soldi

Pause.

BOY: er in WW2. I felt brave and good. Strong enough
         to kiss you. Now I don't need that anymore. I don't
         have to shoot anyone, before I kiss you. It's morning
         and

Pause.

BOY: you're just there. I turn around to you and kiss you.

The BOY turns around. The GIRL is gone. He sits up. Looks around.
Is desperate.

All of a sudden, he gets up, walks over to the bin. Roots through it.
He grabs something – and beams.
He pulls his hand from the bin – and is holding a pair of chicken
drumstick bones.
He smells them. He licks them. He beams. He kisses the bones.
And leaves.

9.

Shortly after Easter.
The BOY is there. He sees the GIRL approach. The BOY hides.
Watches the GIRL. The GIRL looks around. Waits. Looks at the poster.
Then she walks to the phone booth and dials a number.
The BOY's mobile phone rings.

BOY: Yes, hello?

GIRL: Tom?

BOY: Romy?

GIRL: Yes. Where are you?

BOY: In Paris.

Silence.

GIRL: Do you know what happened this morning, when I took the bus from home? I'm sitting on the bus. I look back and see a man, getting beaten up at the bus stop, by a boy and a girl. They kick the man, his stomach, his head, the man is bleeding and doubled over, again an again, the stomach, the head, they don't stop. And then, the bus turns at the intersection, and I see the man's face, very briefly, and I realize that it's my dad.

Silence.

GIRL: You still there?

BOY: Yes.

GIRL: You're not saying anything.

BOY: And what did you do next?

GIRL: I wanted to jump up and stop the bus.
But then I just stayed in my seat. And didn't do anything.
I just carried on.

Silence.

GIRL: And then I realized something else.

BOY: What's that?

GIRL: You know what the girl looked like,
the one who beat up the man?

Silence.

GIRL: Like me.

Silence.

BOY: You should play Tetris.

GIRL: What?

BOY: Oh, nothing.

Silence.

GIRL: It would be nice if you were with me now.

BOY: Is that what you want?

GIRL: Yes. That you take me into your arms. Hold me tight.
I want to feel alive.

The BOY approaches the GIRL.

GIRL: Tom.

Silence. The BOY turns off his mobile.

BOY: Why?

GIRL: What?

BOY: Why were you gone all of a sudden the other day?

GIRL: Me?

BOY: Yes. Sometimes I've asked myself if you were ever
even there.

GIRL: When? Where?

BOY: In Paris. Don't you remember?
Our picnic?

GIRL: Picnic in Paris?

BOY: You brought chicken drumsticks. Haute-cuisine.

GIRL: I've never been to Paris.

BOY: It wasn't really Paris. But almost.
We had a great view over the Eiffel Tower.
Do you remember?

GIRL: No.

Silence.

BOY: You told me about your dream. Where your mum and dad sit at the Greek restaurant and argue about your name.

GIRL: Yes, I do have that dream from time to time. And I told you about it?

BOY: Yes.

GIRL: I've never told anyone about that.

Silence.

BOY: And what about these?

The BOY shows the GIRL some of the chicken bones.

GIRL: Eeeeww. What's this all about?

BOY: They're your bones.
            The bones from the chicken you brought along. You really don't remember?

GIRL: Remember what?

Silence.

GIRL: What's up?

BOY: Kiss me.

GIRL: I have to go.

BOY: Kiss me.

GIRL: My bus.

The GIRL leaves.

BOY: Kiss me!

Silence. The BOY throws away the bones.

BOY: Kiss me. I want to feel that you're alive.

The BOY rips the poster off.
And leaves.

10.

Summertime.
The BOY arrives and sits down. He looks around. Then he looks at a
spot next to him and speaks. As if the GIRL was there.

BOY: Hey. I've thought about us.
And you know what I've realized?
You… you never kissed me. Not once.
I've always been the one to kiss you. Always.
All eigh

Pause.

BOY: teen.

Silence.

BOY: Over the past few weeks I kept asking myself what
that meant.
First I thought, maybe you're too shy, like me.
Then I thought, maybe you're playing the diva

Pause.

BOY: the one who never kisses and always just lets herself
be kissed. And sometimes I lay in
bed and couldn't get off to sleep because I constantly
had that

Pause.

BOY: thought going around in my head, that you maybe
didn't really… well, didn't really want… and in the
end I googled it. 'Why girls don't kiss' , that's what I

Pause.

BOY: searched for. And then I got about 772,000 results.
772,000 answers for why girls don't kiss. I wouldn't
have thought that girls had that many reasons, not to

Pause.

BOY: kiss.

Silence.

BOY: So every day I checked tons and tons of results.
       When I finally got to answer ca 4,012, I came across
       the only correct answer. Do you know why you don't
       kiss

Pause.

BOY: me? You know, do you know why you weren't there
       in Paris with me? You know why you didn't recognise
       those bones, your bones? You know

Pause.

BOY: why?

The GIRL arrives.

BOY: Because you don't exist.

Silence.

BOY: You don't exist.
       That's how easy it is.

Silence.

*The GIRL is there. But the BOY doesn't realize it. He just keeps on
talking to himself.*

BOY: Are you surprised?

GIRL: No.

BOY: You've always known, haven't you?

GIRL: Yes.

BOY: Wouldn't it have been fairer if you'd told me from
        the start?

GIRL: Didn't I?

BOY: Maybe you did. Someone who hasn't got a mobile
        number or an email address, simply can't exist.
        But I wanted you to be real.

GIRL: Thanks.
        No one's ever said that to me before.

Silence.

BOY: For one-and-a-half years I thought I had a girlfriend. My parents never believed me when I told them about you. Why don't you invite her over some time, they

Pause.

BOY: said. And then they said: You're spending too much time in front of the computer, they said. And I always answered: Bus stop. But now I know: You're just an

Pause.

BOY: invention of mine. You don't exist. I'm all on my own here, correct? I should go and play Tetris, that helps. Tetris helps with traumatic experiences. I have co

Pause.

BOY: llected all the news stories that say something positive about computers and computer games. Scientists from the University of Oxford have discovered that play

Pause.

GIRL: I…

BOY: ing Tetris prevents the brain from storing the horrific pictures of a traffic accident, for example, or of badly injured people. If you play Tetris within the f

Pause.

BOY: irst six hours of the event, the storing of these horrific images and creation of memories is prevented. The part of the brain that stores images is instead pre

Pause.

GIRL: …am not real.

BOY: occupied with the turning and twisting of those colourful, geometric shapes in the game. So the brain

is distracted and it prevents bad memories. Cool, isn't
it?

Pause.

BOY: You can read up on it for example on www.netdoctor.
at/nachrichten/?id=120080. I played Tetris on that
Easter night, in order to forget you. And as you can
see,

Pause.

BOY: it worked.

Silence.

GIRL: Don't worry, that's nothing to do with your computer
games. Do you know why I don't exist? Because
my dad never wanted a child. My mum was forever
pressurizing him. But my dad didn't want to.
He refused. Until they weren't even having sex
anymore. And then they split up.
You know, that's why I'm so annoyed at my dad.
He prevents me. He doesn't want me to exist.
And that's why I sometimes beat him up, just like
that.

BOY: I no longer think about you at all. Not for a second.

GIRL: Sometimes my temper just gets the better of me.
Then I just can't help myself. The whole lust for life
comes out. Then I want to: be. Completely normal.
Meet a boy, go on dates, kiss him. But at some point
there always comes that moment when the boy
notices that I don't exist. And that hurts, of course.
And believe you me, I really don't enjoy hurting you
guys all the time. That's why I always vanish when it
gets serious. When it starts being beautiful.
When you're in Paris. You remember.
How I'd love to kiss you! To kiss you! But I can't.
I can't. I can't.

Silence.

The GIRL leaves.

BOY: You know, we've known each other eighteen months now. Usually this would be the right moment for he first…

Silence.

BOY: May I…?

The BOY kisses in the air.

BOY: One.

Silence.

At some point the BOY's phone rings.

BOY: Yes, hello. – Yes, that's mine. – What? Who are you? – You… That's impossible. – You… you are the girl in my poster? That… – Yes, I know, the photo is pretty blurry. But you recognized yourself. – Yes, that's the most important thing. – Of course we can meet, sure! When? Where? – Tomorrow at 3 at the bus stop? – Yes, that's fine by me. – No, I haven't got anything better planned. – Well, see you tomorrow then! Err, what… *(Notices the call has been terminated.)*… 's your name?

The BOY leaves.

WWW.OBERONBOOKS.COM

Follow us on www.twitter.com/@oberonbooks
& www.facebook.com/OberonBooksLondon